Born in 1933, Courtney John Lyndhurst Jones to
ice as a four-year old at the famous Westover Ice
hometown of Bournemouth, Dorset. Having inhe
artistic and musical talents and mutual passion for
knew from an early age that he wanted to be a dres   ...... Also a
keen dancer, in his teens he attained Gold Star medals in both
Ballroom Dancing and Latin American; and translating his skills to
ice, achieved a total of two Silver and nine Gold Medals in the British,
European and World Figure Skating Championships with two
successive partners, June Markham, (1955 – 58), and Doreen Denny,
(1958 – 61). Both partnerships were also awarded the National
Skating Association (NSA) coveted Vandervell Trophy.

After retiring from competition in 1961, Courtney simultaneously
pursued successful careers as a fashion designer in London and a
national and international judge, referee, member of the International
Skating Union (ISU) and NSA Councils, and President of the latter.
In 1980 he received an OBE, (Officer of the Most Excellent Order of
the British Empire), for services to ice skating, and was inducted into
the World Figure Skating Hall of Fame in 1986. Courtney also
received an ISU Georg Hasler Medal in recognition of his
contribution to the sport in 1991, and was appointed as an Honorary
Member of the ISU on his retirement from office in 2010.

Courtney now lives in Spain with his lifelong companion Robert
(Bobby) Thompson, where he mainly encounters ice in the form of
cubes surrounded by a glass of gin and tonic.

1937: With my first skating coach, Kay Simcock, at the window of Westover Ice Rink, Bournemouth, overlooking the sea

COURTNEY JONES

****

AROUND THE ICE IN EIGHTY YEARS:

AN IRREVERENT MEMOIR BY AN ACCIDENTAL CHAMPION

By Courtney Jones, OBE

Compiled and edited by Helen Cox

First published in 2021 by Herstory Writing & Interpretation/
York Publishing Services
R.R.P. £9.99

ISBN 978-0-9928514-3-9

Front cover photo: First steps on ice, 1937: Courtney Jones at Westover Ice
Rink, aged four
Back cover photo: Courtney Jones (right) and Bobby Thompson (left) today
Cover design: Helen Cox & Elaine Hooper

Photographic Acknowledgements: Unless otherwise stated, all
photographs are from the author's private collection. Robin Cousins, MBE,
kindly supplied a portrait from his own collection, and Phil Christensen the
image of Jayne Torvill, OBE, and Christopher Dean, OBE, reproduced with
the generous permission of photographer Alfie Hitchcock. Elsewhere, every
effort has been made to trace/obtain permission from copyright holders,
(the author and publisher are indebted to Paul Dean and Elaine Hooper for
their valuable assistance in this respect); and where this has not been
possible, the photographers' work is hereby gratefully acknowledged.

Printed by:

York Publishing Services,
64, Hallfield Road,
Layerthorpe,
York YO31 7ZQ
Telephone enquiries: 01904 431213
Email enquiries: enqs@yps-publishing.co.uk
Website: www.yps-publishing.co.uk

Order from: www.YPD-books.com

Herstory Writing & Interpretation
www.herstorywriting.com

THIS BOOK IS DEDICATED TO:

JUNE MARKHAM AND DOREEN DENNY
LAWRENCE DEMMY, MBE
INEZ AND REGINALD JONES
JAYNE TORVILL, OBE, AND CHRISTOPHER DEAN,
OBE

Contents:

Foreword

We have known Courtney Jones for forty-five years. We began our relationship with him as young teenagers seeking his advice and assistance, and we now find ourselves many years later as very mature parents of young adults.

When we first met Courtney, he was an elite Ice Dance Judge for Great Britain. We were very young, shy, and certainly intimidated by him as he was the most influential judge in our sport nationally. We were not to know at that first meeting that our lives would become entwined, and that he would become a great mentor, confidant, and trusted friend.

Courtney in his own ice dance career had reached the pinnacle of our sport and become World Champion with two different partners. He was an innovator in ice dance and led the way in bringing style and creativity to the sport. We were fortunate that he took us under his wing and passed on his knowledge and expertise to us freely.

It became clear from the beginning of our relationship that Courtney had the gift of seeing possibilities. We believe that he saw the potential in us, and we had long conversations about ideas, concepts and direction. This was the spark that gave me and Jayne the confidence to begin to think for ourselves and believe in our own ideas and abilities. As we developed our own style of work and creativity, Courtney gently guided and supported us on our journey.

It would be impossible not to include Bobby Thompson, Courtney's lifelong partner, when revisiting these wonderful memories of what was our very small circle of trusted confidants. Bobby was flamboyant, the Yin to the very proper and refined Yang of Courtney. They worked amazingly together. In combination, they really did help us come out of our shells and feel able to flourish.

Courtney and Bobby were influential not only in our careers, but also in the careers of so many other ice dancers. We think that those of us who have known Courtney for many years will all be surprised at the insights into the man we gain from this wonderful autobiography.

Courtney has worked tirelessly as an ambassador and advocate for ice dancing internationally for most of his life. As you read this honest and warm account of his life, we hope that you will find it as inspiring as we have.

Thank you, Courtney, for your love and friendship.

Photograph by Alfie Hitchcock, © Alfie Hitchcock, courtesy of Phil Christensen

Christopher Dean and Jayne Torvill

Introduction: Life's Rich Tapestry

When you start to remember, you hear a chorus of forgotten voices
that lift your heart

Now in my ninth decade and before the permafrost sets in,
I've decided to record some memories I've kept on ice all these years.

On a June day in 2019, long before the dreaded tentacles of
Covid-19 began to engulf every part of our lives and perhaps always
will, I was sitting on the terrace of our home in Spain in the brilliant
sunshine and started to remember, (as old men do), all the wonderful
things life had given me, as well as the low points.

As all these memories crowded in, I began to think that they
might be of interest to those who would follow, and even worth
writing down – so I did! Inspired by Alan Bennett's diaries and *Untold
Stories*, which I was reading at the time, I tackled my brand-new
project by trying to emulate his fluid style, as if talking directly to the
reader. I just hope my other literary idols Oscar Wilde and Noel
Coward were perched on my shoulders as I wrote, lending a hand!

You, dear Reader, must decide whether I succeeded.
Whatever your verdict, I enjoyed every minute as, week by week,
month by month, my written record grew. So many memories, happy
and sad, have made up the tapestry of my life. So many friends, (and a
few enemies!), are woven into the narrative, all influencing me for
good or ill, teaching me many lessons, and helping me make sense of
what was happening at times. It would be impossible to mention
everyone, so if names are omitted, please forgive me. Lack of space
will be the only reason – thank you for your friendship just the same.

To begin, I would like to introduce you to some of these
wonderful people. Naturally, first is my partner of sixty years, Robert
(Bobby) Thompson. For many years, our friendship could not be
officially recognised. Now, thanks to the amazing changes that have
taken place in recent decades, like so many others we no longer need
to hide it and can enjoy the rest of our lives unfettered by the

problems of the past. As I write these reminiscences he is at my side, correcting my lapses of memory and awful spelling, and acting as my unpaid live-in editor. He has, at last, found his *raison d'être* and is, as usual, my rock! More of him later.

Two glittering golden threads woven throughout are my leading ladies, without whom I would never have had such a life in skating. Obviously, if you want to compete as a pairs skater or ice dancer, the one thing you can't manage without is a partner - and in my championship career I've been blessed with two absolute world beaters, completely different in temperament but completely alike in dedication, discipline, and in the way our talents combined and complemented one another. So I'll always be greatly indebted to June Markham and Doreen Denny for allowing me to be their partner and for staying good friends with me for all these years. More of them later, too.

Talking of life's 'characters,' Yvonne Mango was at the top of that tree, (a very nice one)! We met through our connections with ballroom dancing, where she was a fixture throughout her life. 'Everyone' knew Yvonne as the most entertaining company and one of the kindest people we'd ever met. The daughter of a society portrait artist, she had met many famous people in her life and was married to Alec Mango, an actor best known for his role in the *Hornblower* TV series, although he also starred in many films and his co-stars always ended up as Yvonne's friends rather than his! (She loved talking about her famous friends). Alec always made sure in his contracts that Yvonne could travel with him wherever he was filming all over the world; and Yvonne always dressed, at any time of the day, as if she had just left a party or was on her way to one. To her, chiffon was the ideal fabric to go to get the groceries, and she was usually to be seen shopping in the local MacFisheries at Notting Hill Gate at nine in the morning, arrayed in long eyelashes teamed with a cocktail dress, high heels, and enough bling to stock a Bond Street jeweller's shop. Everyone knew and loved her. She was so popular.

We first met Yvonne at Josephine Bradley's Dance Studio in

South Kensington. (Miss Bradley, the foremost Ballroom Adjudicator in the world and inventor of the modern Foxtrot, was still travelling to the USA to lecture well into her nineties. She kindly included us in the parties that followed the dance evenings in her studio, which were always great fun and we met many of our friends in the ballroom world there). When we got to know Yvonne, she and Alec lived opposite the Russian Embassy in W2, and one cold morning there was a group of women demonstrating about human rights in Russia when she tripped downstairs in her usual totally unsuitable outfit. As she was crossing the road, one of the demonstrators shouted, "Would you like to be under a man?" Yvonne replied, "Darling, I can't think of anything better," and merrily went on her way.

Times weren't always easy for the Mangos, and they had one room stuffed with antiques from much better days – like Queen Mary's bed and her father's paintings, and the menu for the last banquet held by Tsar Nicholas II before he was deposed, among numerous other treasures which, as their financial situation deteriorated, went off to auction one by one. Yvonne continued to be a dear friend until she passed away some years ago. In her will she left us the silver goblets she always used for her many parties, ("Never glasses, my dear!"), and they remain a lovely reminder of the happy times we spent in her company.

The Ronaldson family have also been stalwart friends and helpers over many decades. At the head was their matriarch, May, who only left the stage in her nineties some years ago. Born in Bovey Tracey, south Devon, she was a member of a travelling family who lived in what she called a 'wagon,' and brought up her family as they travelled all over the country organizing fairs.

May addressed everyone from princess to pauper as 'my dear' in her wonderful Devonshire accent, (she did have other names for people she didn't like, but let's not go into those!). Travellers, she always pointed out, were not Gypsies, and had a strict code of conduct she adhered to until she died. It was not until she took charge of the Festival of Britain Funfair in London's Battersea Park that she and the family finally capitulated and moved into a large house on Battersea Roundabout, abandoning the wagon. The house was always full of friends listening to May dispense her undoubted wisdom, while her sister, aged over a hundred, remained in Devon in charge of her own local shooting range. They were an indomitable family.

Immaculate until the end of her life, May never appeared other than beautifully dressed and coiffured, except that she never carried a handbag; doing the work she did, she kept her change in her pocket ready to shake hands on any deal that was offered her. As head of the family, she decided where each funfair stall was to be situated on the field, with family in the centre and newcomers on the perimeter. Interestingly, when Billy Butlin left the National Service May gave him a site to start him off, and we all know how successful he became! He never forgot her kindness and always kept in touch during his march to the top as magnate of the popular Butlin's Holiday Camps.

This typified May. She was kindness personified if she liked you, but Lord help you if she didn't! She had a wide range of suggestions where you could go in that case, accompanied by some choice language usually incorporating the letter F.

During May's 'reign' at Wembley we had a rather interesting occasion when the National Skating Association (NSA) was hosting a charity ice gala and the guest of honour was Princess Alexandra, cousin of the Queen. Naturally, once the gala was announced, the seating in the Royal Box and the guests in the Royal Retiring Room became very hot topics. The President and older members of the Council had strict ideas as to who was suitable for the honour, and at one early meeting when decisions were being taken, I tentatively suggested May. Shock horror! That was not a suitable name for such an auspicious occasion, and it was turned down flat.

On Gala night, I realised May was very upset not to be included, although she didn't show it. The evening started as planned with the arrival of the Princess, a most charming and natural guest and very interesting to talk to. I was seated beside her, and as the proceedings began, she asked me, "Where's May?"

What a *faux pas*! I quickly passed a note along the front row to get someone to alert May – she was needed in the interval. As the note passed, the people's faces were a picture and I sat there and gloated.

When the first half finished, we all rose to escort the Princess to the Retiring Room for refreshments and there was May, looking fantastic as always. Without any ceremony, she flung her arms around Princess Alexandra, said, "Hullo, my darling," and kissed her.

The VIPs nearly fainted as they chatted away like old friends, the Princess telling May about her children, and taking the gifts she'd brought for 'the kids.' What these posh people didn't realise was that, as May ran all the concession stalls around the concourse, she had met Princess Alexandra many times, got on with her like a house on fire, and for many years had been giving her 'kids' gifts each time they came for a function.

On another occasion, May was standing at the top of the steps leading up to her tall house on Battersea Roundabout in carpet slippers and overall, watching an obviously important personage being escorted over the bridge by police outriders. Suddenly it all drew to a halt outside her house. The limousine's window was wound down. Princess Alexandra's head poked out. "May!" she shouted.

May went down the steps, stuck her head into the car and they had a chat before the entourage proceeded on to wherever they were bound – a little story indicative of the affection in which May was held by one and all, and the effect she had with her warm heart, natural exuberance, and love of life in general – qualities inherited by her daughter Chloe, a World Champion Roller Speed skater who features as an All-Time Great in the *Guinness Book of Records* because no-one has ever surpassed her record for winning world titles in her chosen sport.

(In those days there was a very close relationship between ice figure-skaters, speed skaters, and their opposite numbers in roller skating. All the parties, dances, and galas always included helpers from both disciplines, and we always attended each other's major events; the camaraderie between us was the mainstay of our sports. Sadly, that friendship no longer exists due to what I call the 'nationalisation' of ice and roller skating by the Government some thirty years ago. Now sporting organizations only exist with the help of central and National Lottery funds, with the aim of encouraging youngsters as well as older people to learn to skate; but the schemes to achieve international success are so badly planned and funded that this is rarely, if ever, achieved. Excepting the speed skaters, compared with our previous successes, today's lack speaks for itself, and will not change until the mindset of those in charge completely alters. More of *that* later, too!).

Another two precious threads are a wonderful lady and her husband, from whom we could all learn about how to live life to the full and overcome insuperable problems. Peggy Roth was tiny, but mighty as a lion in her approach to life. She skated at Queens Ice Club in London, loved dancing on ice, and was still skiing well into her eighties. She also rode, took part in Spanish dancing, played tennis, and in between, cared for all the friends who looked to her for comfort and advice. She and her husband Pepe lived in a large Victorian house in Maida Vale, north-west London, where they took in lodgers she looked after as if they were family, and the story of their lives was like a film script.

Peggy was born into a prosperous Jewish family, and just before the start of World War Two was living in Vienna, Austria. With the storm clouds gathering, her parents became very conscious of their plight, and decided to send their two daughters and son to live in the UK. This wasn't easy, but Peggy managed to get to London in the guise of a ladies' maid; her siblings also succeeded in escaping, and their parents promised to follow. Sadly, this was not to happen, and the last time any of them saw their mother and father was waving goodbye at the railway station – both later perished in the Nazi death camps.

When she moved to London, Peggy had no experience other than in sewing; hence she reinvented herself as a corsetiere and built up a large clientele, especially with the upper classes. After the war she married Pepe and they had a daughter, Tatiana, who would go on to marry a top music producer and live in Hollywood, California. Peggy often went out there to visit her daughter and her family and

Dear friends:

Left: Yvonne Mango

Below: Peggy and Pepe Roth

was the much-loved star at all their gatherings.

Pepe, who spoke many languages, had been imprisoned in Ukraine at the beginning of the war, and suffered torture. He was also imprisoned in the notorious Lubyanka Prison in Moscow but managed to escape. This escape was the stuff of thriller magazines: he was told to go to a railway station and a man would hand him a newspaper, in which would be a ticket that would take him to the Czech border where, as the train slowed over a mountain pass, he was to jump and make his way to the first of a number of safe houses throughout Czechoslovakia and then across the border into Switzerland and safety.

He never forgot the kindness he received, and annually returned to see his saviours and tell them, once more, of his appreciation. Pepe went on to become Political Correspondent at one of the top newspapers. He and Peggy were the most wonderful company, with so many tales to tell – an incredible couple from whom it was possible to learn so much about what's important in life.

The epitome of indomitable, Peggy never changed, keeping going even as she was losing her sight – and would've done so for much longer, had she not fallen outside her home and never recovered. After her funeral, we all retired to a local hotel and had a wonderful, hilarious afternoon recalling all the fun times we had spent in her company. Like Peggy herself, her funeral was like no other, and so happy – exactly how she would have wanted.

A very special thread in my tapestry is Eileen Anderson, one of those skating characters on whom everyone depended. Simply, for as long as I can remember she was there, whatever the project and however difficult the odds, offering help and advice.

Eileen was a social skater before the war, a member of the Wembley Skating Club, and a very close friend of Reg Wilkie, a past British Ice Dance Champion with Daphne Wallis. (On the recommendation of the NSA Figure Committee, a special committee was set up to study ice dancing, resulting in the discipline gaining its first official recognition in 1933. The first official British Ice Dance Championships, won by Daphne Wallis and Reg Wilkie, took place in

1939. The 1937 and 1938 competitions were called The National Ice Dance Competition, both won by Reg and Daphne, and re-designated as the British Ice Dance Championship after 1939).

Reg went on to become very active in the growth of the sport and is often referred to as 'the father of modern ice dancing.' In turn this recognition led to the first International Skating Union (ISU) World Ice Dance Championships being held in Paris, France, in 1952, when the winners were Lawrence Demmy and Jean Westwood; and the first European Championships in Bolzano, Italy, in 1954 – also won by Lawrence and Jean, who went on to add a total of four World and two European titles to their string of successes.

Eileen's closeness to Reg, and the help she gave him in setting out the rules and regulations, meant that she became an integral part of the skating scene. Never married, Eileen had a distinguished business career as the personal assistant and secretary to the managing director of Fred Olsen, the shipping line based in Regent Street, London. She held the post until she retired, when she was honoured to have a ship named after her. This unusual honour was celebrated by a very lavish dinner, on board, before the official launch. I was delighted to be asked to accompany her, but foolishly felt seasick even though it was anchored in Tilbury Docks, east of London, (I only really like water iced, in a glass)!

After the war, as things returned to normal, Eileen began to take part in organizing events for the NSA Ice Dance Committee, where she showed her great organizational abilities. In those days the headquarters staff consisted only of a General Secretary, Roger Drake, (preceded by Eric Coggins), and a couple of secretaries; everything else was done by amateur enthusiasts, and Eileen was always there to advise and assist. By the time I was elected Chairman of the Ice Dance Committee, Eileen had become Secretary, and with the help of a very active committee, we took great pleasure in bringing the discipline into greater prominence over the next two decades. Then when other projects and other committees were created, somehow Eileen, with her great knowledge of the sport, was still there to help. A very fast typist with excellent shorthand, she was perfect for us all to lean on – and lean we did!

Graduating to Team Leader for the various events abroad, Eileen proved to be a cross between Mother Hen and Hitler, (come to think of it, an ideal combination for the job). She was Team Leader when John Curry and Robin Cousins won their Olympic Golds; and perhaps the crowning moment of her career, in 1984 when Torvill and Dean won their Gold Medals in front of the largest audience ever seen for ice dancing. Her picture was seen by millions of people worldwide, greeting Jayne and Chris as they left the ice.

Certainly, throughout my career on ice and subsequently as an organizer of international events including the 1989 European Championships and 1995 World Championships, Eileen was always there for me; I owe her a special debt of gratitude for her unbelievable contribution to our sport, as well as to me personally. Happily, this contribution was recognised by Her Majesty the Queen with an OBE, and by the International Olympic Committee's special badge for outstanding members of the international sporting community, towards the end of her career.

During its halcyon years, British skating was dominated from the other side of the barrier in the nicest possible way by a triple thread I call the 'Three Graces.' These three strong lady officials were all highly motivated to improving the sport in the UK and. even more importantly, abroad. All three were highly qualified in solo skating, pairs skating and ice dancing, and all three were not poor - in fact, quite the opposite - but their words and advice were always listened to with politeness and had an enormous effect on the growth of our sport although, at the time, we didn't always realise their contribution.

Pamela Davis was a Gold Medallist turned judge, referee, and international judge, in all three branches of the sport, giving her the best possible credentials to opine on everything to do with skating. A very elegant woman, Pamela was always immaculately dressed and, in those days, swathed in wonderful furs. The daughter of a diamond merchant, she had married the extremely handsome owner of a chain of silver shops; they soon became darlings of the gossip columns and were rarely out of the society magazines, with photos always appearing of them sunning themselves in St Moritz, Monaco, and the

South of France.

Pam exuded an aura of wealth, and the fact that she knew her job as far as skating was concerned gave candidates for medal tests quaking knees as soon as she appeared! I first met her in 1947 when she arrived at Westover Ice Rink, my home rink, as one of the judges for a moderately low-level test, and I knew nothing of her reputation. (By the way, I failed, as I did nearly every test level I ever attempted before succeeding. A salutary lesson: don't give up at the first hurdle. You can make it if you persevere!). Little did I realise, on that sunny afternoon, what part this woman would play in my skating life. Years later she became my advisor and dearest friend, but still the most ardent critic when I began to compete. Her advice was always right, but not necessarily accepted with the good grace it should have been!

Over the decades to follow I had so many ventures to raise money for skaters and Pam was there to advise and help. She had an apartment just behind Harvey Nichols and I value the many happy hours I spent there despite our many, many fallings out. We always thought we were right and the other not, and sometimes didn't speak for months on end, but like true friends we always made up.

Sadly, she lost her husband to illness after a very short marriage and mourned for him for the rest of her life, (though she never showed it). In memory of her husband, she instigated the John Davis Trophies for top-class ice dance couples, and when you look at the list of annual winners it's interesting to note the international success nearly every one of the dancers who have their name engraved on it achieved. The first winners in 1961 were Linda Shearman and Michael Phillips; other notables include the late Janet Sawbridge, who won it with David Hickinbottom in 1963, 1964 and 1965, with Jon Lane in 1966, 1967 and 1968, and on three more occasions in the Seventies with Peter Dalby; four-time winners Janet Thompson and Warren Maxwell; and, in 1978 and 1979, Jayne Torvill and Christopher Dean.

Pam then turned her attention to improving the sport. She was already an International Referee, and it was always so comforting to have her on the panel as we skaters always knew she would judge us fairly, and her comments after each event were crucial to our advance to the top. Pam gave her life to the sport and was awarded with a well-deserved MBE. Unfortunately, towards the end she descended into dementia, but was cared for until the last with enormous love and dedication by another UK member of the ISU, Mrs Helen Poole. Pam passed away peacefully in her own home and so ended an era that will never return to our sport.

Out to dinner with Pamela Davie (right) and Bobby Thompson (left), photograph courtesy of Helen Volguchev

Mollie Phillips, OBE, was another 'character' in our sport. She also was qualified in all branches of skating and judged and officiated all over the world. Just before World War Two was declared she had recently qualified as a barrister, but did not take Silk, and lived in a three-hundred-year-old apartment in Lincoln's Inn, on the edge of the City of London. A very astute, albeit eccentric, official, it was always fun to have Mollie around. Engaged to a fighter pilot sadly killed early in the conflict, she never married but made her life in skating, as well as being appointed High Sheriff of Carmarthenshire, south-west Wales, the first woman ever appointed to this prestigious post.

A member of the British Team in the 1932 Winter Olympics held at Lake Placid in the Adirondacks, New York, Mollie was placed ninth in the Ladies' Individual Skating, just behind Cecilia Colledge in eighth place. Moreover, she was the first female to ever carry her nation's flag at the opening ceremony for this or any other Games, Winter or Summer, making her particularly memorable in Olympic circles. Mollie was also the first female to be elected to an NSA committee and the first female to referee an ISU Championship. All her skating costumes were made by Norman Hartnell, the Queen's dress designer, and before she died, I helped her pick out a number of them, superbly made, for her to present to the United States Hall of Fame, (now the World Figure Skating Museum), so they wouldn't disappear forever from the worldwide skating scene.

Through her contacts, Mollie helped the NSA to have its offices moved into the Charterhouse, some of the most prestigious and historical offices in central London, where the organization resided for some years. Even as her health deteriorated in later life, she still attended all the skating events she possibly could, finally meeting her end in her nineties when she fell and hit her head ascending the centuries-old winding staircase in her apartment in Lincoln's Inn after attending a party. It was just the way she would've wanted to leave for the big ice rink in the sky - she really loved a party! Good for Mollie! Cheers!

My third 'Grace,' Pauline Borrajo, was a very interesting skater turned International Referee and Judge after a long and distinguished career on ice as a British Ice Dance Champion with her partner Sonny Edmonds. I first saw her in 1947 when she and her partner came to give exhibitions at the Westover Ice Rink. Little did I know that she would play a part in my success a decade later, when she was judging International and British Ice Dance events. A great friend and past pupil of my own coach, mentor, and friend Miss Gladys Hogg, she was always on hand to give advice and became a close friend. (When the first ever TV show on ice was staged from Queens Ice Club, Miss Hogg paired us together as the lead couple in a Latin American Dance number, with me wearing the most appalling sombrero). Pauline's knowledge and insight were immense; she contributed a great deal to the advancement of the art of Ice Dancing and sat on many of the committees formed in later years by the NSA.

The arrival of these three ladies, often together, at any skating competition or Championships struck fear in the hearts of the competitors! Their names may not have much resonance with today's skaters, but they nonetheless had a huge influence on the growth of post-war skating; into the Sixties, when British competitive skaters of their era moved into coaching across the world, particularly Canada and the USA; and on into the Nineties as judges, referees and NSA committee members. The basic tenets of the techniques learnt in those early years thus became the foundation of teaching worldwide – so the names of Pamela Davis, Mollie Phillips and Pauline Barrajo should not be forgotten but hailed as they deserve, as great pioneers of our sport.

(By an odd quirk of fate, in 2005 we moved into Bedford House in The Avenue, Chiswick, west London. Built in 1793, it was the oldest house in Chiswick and once the home of John Linley, one of the founders of the nearby Royal Botanic Gardens at Kew. Bedford House had a Blue Plaque on the wall outside advertising his past residency and was still surrounded by gardens containing many exotic plants and covering a large area of the environs, now Bedford Park. Interestingly, the soldiers and officers on their way to the Battle of Waterloo had practiced their firing ability in the garden of Bedford House before leaving to fight in France in 1815).

When we moved in, the building had been transformed into twelve different apartments. From our windows we were able to see the block in which both Miss Hogg and Pauline had occupied two different flats - another skating connection! Added to which, a local historian who came to see us said that Florence Madeline 'Madge' Syers, who came second in the 1902 World Figure Skating Championships, had also lived in The Avenue. In Madge's time, the event was held at an indoor ice rink called Henglers Circus, better known today as the London Palladium in Oxford Circus. (By yet another strange coincidence, many years ago I bought an antique mirror in a country house sale. When I got it home and started to dismantle it in order to repaint the frame, I found the mirror had a backing of old newspapers, in one of which was a large advert for Henglers Circus).

The World Championships were meant for men, but as it hadn't occurred to anyone that a lady would enter, there was no rule to prevent it – a loophole Madge boldly exploited. The IEV, (then initials of the ISU, as the title wasn't in English), were horrified that she entered - much less came second! - and at the next Congress, passed a rule prohibiting female contestants. Madge and her husband then fought a very hard campaign, against fierce resistance, for a separate Ladies Championship to be introduced. She went on to win the first World Ladies Championship in 1906 and again in 1907, and became the Olympic Champion at the 1908 Olympic Games, the first to include figure skating, where she also won Bronze competing in the pairs event with her husband, Edgar Syers. Other female World Champions to follow in her illustrious footsteps were Herma Szabo and Sonja Henie, who controversially won the 1927 title in Oslo, Norway, when three partisan Norwegian judges outvoted the Austrian and German judges to place her first and Szabo second – prompting a new rule that no more than one judge per country could sit on the judging panel.

A man not known to everyone in person but who has become an important cog in our organization is Fredi Schmid, the Director General of the ISU. This man, whom I am proud to call a friend as well as a colleague, is well known to all who participate in the events, but who works quietly behind the scenes. It was in 1996 that Fredi took over from his predecessor, Beat Hasler, as General Secretary, and in 2006 he was named as the Director General, an office he has held ever since, serving under two consecutive Presidents with great distinction.

Fredi's knowledge, after all these years of association with our sport, is encyclopaedic. No question is too large or too small, and he's adept at answering them all with speed and great politeness. His rather stern exterior masks a man with a great sense of humour which he always uses to calm the situation if things begin to get difficult. My story would not be complete without a mention of the great times we've enjoyed together and Fredi's great service to the sport. It's not often that I have such an opportunity to publicly thank Fredi for the many kindnesses he has shown me, personally, through the years. The ISU is lucky to have such a knowledgeable and urbane man of infinite patience to be there for us all, supported by his equally patient staff in the Headquarters in Lausanne.

The final thread of this tapestry of love and appreciation is a person who came independently into both of our lives, amazingly at about the same time, (some sixty-five years ago), and at opposite ends of the country. His name is a legend in skating circles: Lawrence Demmy.

When Bobby was a youngster, he loved to watch skaters and ballet dancers on TV, longing in his heart to emulate their prowess. However, he came from a staunch football family, and that was the only sport to be considered under any circumstances. In fact, Bobby's elder brother tried out for a Manchester football club, but his hopes were dashed through unexpected illness, and his goal of being a footballer was never achieved. So the idea that the younger son could be involved in a 'pastime,' (not sport), as effeminate as ice skating was beyond the family's belief. His ambitions were certainly not encouraged! Nonetheless, Bobby persevered. To fund his first steps, he took his father's beer bottles back to the pub, and used the returned deposit money to go to the Derby Street Ice Palace; he could only afford the occasional trip, and was bought some skating boots as a gift by his uncle.

Being Bobby, he never let such a small thing as lack of funds stand in his way; while he skated, he used to watch other people having lessons and began to learn that way. At that time, the mid-Fifties, Lawrence Demmy was at the top of his tree and, with Jean Westwood, the current World and European Ice Dance Champions. Lawrence became intrigued by this wide-eyed young man in cheap skates and boots, surreptitiously watching as he trained, started to talk to him, and gave him some tips. Bobby, of course, took these to heart, and to the ice like a duck to water.

As he started work, Bobby spent all his spare cash at the rink and began taking the proficiency tests, coached up to Silver standard by Wendy Mann and Harry Parnell, his strongest influences at the time. Lawrence, with Reg Wilkie, judged this Silver test, choosing the Blues as his solo dance, (it's possible to fail a dance test on the quality of the solo dance). Bobby says that his solo test appeared to last much longer than usual, and to his consternation, he was on a second Blues sequence and convinced that he'd failed when he was called to the barrier to receive the result, and found to his pleasure that he'd passed. Apparently, the judges had enjoyed his solo so much that they'd forgotten to stop him continuing – a great compliment!

It prompted Bobby to take the extreme decision to leave home, move to London, and try and find a partner to compete. Living in a bedsit close to Streatham Ice Rink, he made huge financial sacrifices to skate; and after competing as an amateur for some time, decided to turn professional and teach. He was offered the job of National Ice Dance Coach for the Italian team, and set off for Milan on the Orient Express, (in the back, not the posh part), clutching a packet of sandwiches made by his mother, for a journey literally into the unknown. He didn't speak a word of Italian.

That journey changed his life forever and, as it happened, mine as well, though this was not apparent at the time. I had just completed my last year in competition and, after quitting, had gone to watch the 1962 World Championships in Geneva, Switzerland, with Vi Denny, the mother of my now ex-partner Doreen. I remarked to Vi how much the Italian dance couples had improved since the previous year and asked who trained them. I was dumbfounded to find out it was Bobby. Incidentally, his top couple at that time were Olga Gilardini and Germano Ceccattini, ranked seventh on that occasion; many years later, Olga and I sat on the ISU Dance Committee together, and she has remained a dear friend to both of us ever since.

It was Lawrence who suggested that I, very mixed up and downhearted as I was at the time, continued my judging experience to international level, and acted as my mentor throughout the years that followed. I rose through the ranks of national judging, became a Referee, and went on to judge many events and championships all

Our good friend and colleague Lawrence Demmy with his partner Jean Westwood,
1951 World Ice Dance Champions

over the world before being elected to the ISU Ice Dance Committee in 1992, and to the ISU Council from 2002 until my retirement in 2010.

Throughout these halcyon years, Lawrence was always there to guide me and Bobby; the ISU is a very political organization and looking back, we both agree that neither of us would have achieved what we did without his friendship and guidance. The consummate diplomat, in the skating world he was a bit like Marmite – you either loved or hated him! Most people like sycophants who agree with their point of view. That was certainly not Lawrence's way of working, and he was always the first to support new ideas whatever it cost him in popularity – he really did love the sport of figure skating.

Lawrence, his wife Pam, (though she really didn't enjoy the company of many in our sport), Bobby and I became a formidable team behind the scenes, and Pam and Bobby became particularly close at events around the world. Pam is very elegant and dressed beautifully, with great style, which caused some envy among the other 'ISU Wives' who were not always kind to her, especially when Lawrence lost the Presidency of the ISU in Boston, USA. She faced this disappointment with immense dignity and style, and Pam being Pam, always gave better than she got - which made some ladies even more envious of her.

When Lawrence retired from being Vice-President of the ISU Council, I also retired, and after that the three of us had many happy hours together both on the ice and off. Shortly after we moved to Spain in 2002, he and Pam decided to move from their delightful home in York, the picturesque county town of Yorkshire, and bought an apartment close to where we'd settled in Puerto Banus on the Costa del Sol. From then on, no subject was sacrosanct as far as humour was concerned, and we had all sorts of fun attending many major events together as guests of the ISU, without any responsibilities, and always had a ball as Lawrence's humour was so infectious.

We often laughed about the time we were both suffering from what is politely called piles, as many skaters do – perhaps it's the cold mist rising from the ice and freezing our assets! Anyway, my doctor recommended I pay a visit to an eminent Harley Street specialist about this unfortunate condition. I duly attended my appointment and was examined by said specialist, who recommended a course of treatment which proved very successful. Later, when Lawrence was suffering from the same problem, I immediately suggested he saw the same specialist, and he experienced the same excellent result. Much to our childish sense of humour, we were delighted when the gentleman in question was made Lord Mayor of London, and we could both boast that we'd had a Lord Mayor of London examine parts of our bodies where the sun don't shine!

Sadly, Lawrence is no longer with us. However, he left an undeniable legacy to the sport which had already been recognised with the award of MBE, (Member of the Most Excellent Order of the British Empire), by Her Majesty the Queen, and his name and partnership with Jean Westwood will always number among the greats of figure skating.

Without all these wonderful people I would never have had the life I've enjoyed, and I hope you enjoy my memories of it.

Now let us skate!

Chapter 1: How It All Began

When you fall over, don't make excuses - admit you need to be better

I was born on April 30th, 1933, in a nursing home in Poole, Dorset, as the sun rose over the Purbeck Hills - surprising my mother and everyone else, as my arrival was not expected until a little later.

I received the rather unusual name Courtney, (I have no idea why), plus the names of my respective grandfathers, John and Lyndhurst. However, I shall always be grateful to my parents for calling me something original and, as it turned out, memorable.

As a surname, Courtney may have arrived in England with the conquering Normans who became the Courtney Earls of Devon, or from Ireland as a form of O'Curnain, an Old Irish name meaning 'descendant of Curnan'. It was a male Christian name by 1677, when we had an MP called Sir Courtney Pool, and went unisex in 1956 thanks to Pamela Moore's novel *Chocolates for Breakfast*. Attorney General Robert F. Kennedy presumably enjoyed the book because he named his second daughter, born that same year, after its heroine Courtney Farrell. In the Sixties and Seventies, celebrity Courtneys of both sexes, from athletes to actors and drag queens, cropped up all over North America. The name spread to Britain in the Eighties when the great jazz saxophonist, Courtney Pine, rose to fame; and finally achieved mass appeal in 1995, when the sitcom *Friends*, starring Courtney Cox as Monica, became a smash hit, and two years later when a baby girl in the British soap *EastEnders* was named Courtney – often resulting in total confusion when I completed the 'sex' part on official documents!

The parents who bestowed said unusual name were Mother, born Inez Mary Matilda Willsher, and Father, Reginald Claude Jones. Mother was the daughter of Amelia, a seamstress who travelled all over Britain copying Paris fashions to make for titled ladies, and Lyndhurst, a coal merchant. Their shotgun wedding, and their daughter's unusual name, make me wonder if my real grandfather might have been a Spanish onion seller! Father came from a large family who lived on a smallholding in Church Stretton in Shropshire. Their property, while small, had been in the family for hundreds of years; I still have the pre-sixteenth century deeds describing the family as yeomen, which meant that they farmed their own land, and were obliged in times of war to supply males aged over sixteen to fight in the local lord's army. It rejoiced in the romantic name of Minton Oaks, but is now occupied by others after my father, last heir to the property, sold it in 1950.

Both my parents were very reticent about their upbringing. I believe Father was a self-taught academic, and it was only after he died that I discovered he held a doctorate in Psychology, since he had never mentioned the fact nor used it, (I suppose it wasn't much use when selling cattle food, a substance that simply went in one end and came out the other!). At the beginning of World War One in 1914, he lied about his age (sixteen) to join the Royal Flying Corps, trained to become a pilot, and won his wings. He was just about to be sent to the front in France, (life expectancy six weeks, since the flimsy wooden planes had no parachutes), when it was announced over the loudspeaker system on Waterloo Station that the Armistice had been signed - so he never left our shores, thank goodness.

When the Royal Air Force (RAF) was formed in 1919, Father chose to transfer, but later joined the cattle-food manufacturer J. Bibby and Sons, where he stayed until his retirement. Despite always working as a salesman, Father was a frustrated artist and throughout his life painted and drew very well, encouraging all my artistic endeavours and leaving me many of his watercolours and sketches, which adorn my walls today.

Initially appointed as a partner to another sales representative in Salisbury, Wiltshire, he began his working life in that beautiful city, and would remain in the south of England for the rest of his life. I have no idea how he met Mother, who lived in Braintree, Essex, and was originally employed as a chauffeuse then later ran an employment agency; but I do know from photos that Father was an extremely handsome man, always well turned out, and quite a daring dresser, (he loved clothes); and from letters I found after his death, that he had had a number of other girlfriends before getting married.

However, I imagine Mother's pregnancy brought him to a shuddering stop, and they married just one month before I was born. In those days this was quite shameful, as I was nearly illegitimate; mind you, in subsequent years, the alternative word for being born out of wedlock was the opinion of quite a few skaters I judged! Such a situation ran in the family, as I later found out - Mother was born just one month after her own mother got married - explaining why my parents never celebrated their wedding anniversary, and I never saw any photographs of the happy day.

To general confusion, Father called Mother 'Susie', Mother called Father 'Rex', and I was called 'Sam,' (or 'Junior,' for reasons to be disclosed). In character they were poles apart. Father was very polite, a little introverted, but charming to everyone, (particularly the ladies); an extremely active man who, on top of his long working days, joined my school's board of governors, later becoming Chairman, and somehow still found time for his hobbies of skating - he was keen enough to own his own boots - and art.

Mother was the opposite. A pretty, slightly plump woman, she was very gregarious, loving company and bright clothes which she wore with panache, and joked that she'd like to be a barmaid with dyed blonde hair, (even though she didn't drink apart from the odd glass of wine, while for my father to have a sherry made it a red-letter day). Needless to say, he didn't approve of the idea!

After Father received a promotion, we moved to Bournemouth, (then in Hampshire, now in Dorset), on the south coast, where my parents bought 'Sun Trap,' a new-build bungalow at 9, Kings Avenue, Parkstone, and stayed there for the rest of their lives. (Father passed away aged ninety-seven, having spent only one night in a convalescent home, and Mother died at ninety. Sadly, I was in Canada officiating at a major event when my friend Vanessa Riley, BEM, the now retired International Figure Skating Judge and holder of the British Empire Medal who then lived in Bournemouth, called to say that Mother had been taken into hospital. I called the hospital, learned that she was in a private room, and safe; then spoke to the Matron, who told me that, off her own bat, Mother had rung a hairdresser and refused any further treatment until she'd had her hair and nails done - typical! I was unable to fly back because the airports were shut down due to heavy snow. By the time I got back to the UK, Mother was very poorly, but I did at least see her before she passed - and Vanessa proved what a great friend she was by helping me make all the arrangements because I soon had to return to London. My parents had always been there for me, and in time I was able to return their love and encouragement by making sure their last years were comfortably spent in their own home).

I remember 'Sun Trap' as an attractive residence, and we had a maid who also did the cooking, a part-time gardener, and a company car which Mother was not allowed to drive. Life there could have been idyllic had not my mother, who loved her job, been obliged to give it up because of Father's Victorian belief that wives shouldn't work outside the home. As he was out all day travelling to farms throughout Hampshire and Dorset, this meant she found herself lonely with only a baby for company, no friends, and nothing to do. Luckily, Father soon got a new partner, Basil Bennett, recently married to Connie and with a new-born baby. The Bennetts remained great friends with my parents until the end of their lives, and as Auntie Con and Uncle Basil, became a huge part of my upbringing. Sadly, their only son Brian died in a tragic car accident while he was at university, and they never fully recovered from the loss.

My fifth year would turn out to be one of the most formative of my life. Mother enjoyed playing the piano, and now that I was four, with enough manual strength and dexterity, she suggested I try learning myself. A then-unknown pianist, Robert Keys, who played in one of the bands that in those days entertained the diners in department stores' restaurants, was recruited to teach me. Although I could barely read, Robert came to our house and showed me the rudiments, his enthusiasm fostering the love of music in every form which remains with me to this day. I soon began to enjoy playing and apparently showed some promise, being able to compose simple melodies by the time I was six.

At that point World War Two intervened. After declaring himself a conscientious objector, Robert was given a choice of going

Left: My parents, Reginald 'Rex' and Inez 'Susie' Jones

Below: our family home, 'Sun Trap,' in the snow

to prison or moving to Scotland to do forestry work. He chose the latter and, because of the impending danger, suggested that he and his wife took me with them to train as a concert pianist, as he felt I had the necessary talent. Naturally my parents made sure I stayed with them, but I wonder what course my life would have taken had they acceded to his request? Many years later, Robert became a very famous international pianist, ending as the raconteur at Covent Garden theatre, where we met up once more shortly before he died. His funeral was attended by stars from all over the world.

My life-long love-affair with skating also began in 1937, at the Westover Ice Rink on Bournemouth's premier Westover Road. The rink was a fabulous Art Deco structure with tall, tiered windows giving a delightful sea view, and a large skating scene mural on the wall opposite; it was built on as a first floor to Westover Motors, the car showroom and garage owned by a Major Sharp, primarily so that his children Henry Graham and Heather could learn to skate without having to travel far to a rink. The Major then engaged a Canadian show skater, (Phil Taylor, famous for skating on stilts), to teach them. Graham Sharp, as he was known, learned so well that he won the British Championships five years in succession from 1934, and was also the reigning World Champion when war broke out in 1939.

The rink was an immediate hit with locals when it opened in December 1930, and a popular venue for summer tourists. The first professional ice show, staged by the General Manager John Neal, took place in 1931 and became an annual fixture, with shows like *Arabian Nights* and *Yokohama* playing to packed houses. Ironically, its success meant that when Graham Sharp was practicing for the European and World Championships in 1938, he had to travel after all – thirty-three miles to Southampton - to get an empty rink!

Westover boasted its own full orchestra, led by Percy Pearce, to play during public sessions. These featured breaks when only dance couples could take the ice, and dances including the Ten-step and Kilian Waltzes, Foxtrots, Blues and Quicksteps were played, with all dancers skating the prescribed patterns and steps – incidentally teaching one rink-craft in order to avoid crashing into other couples. Professional staff were paid individually to partner the skaters, which

Above: Westover Ice Rink c.1931, from a postcard by Fred Judge © Judges of Hastings, www.judgesampson.com, *by kind permission of Trevor Wolford*

Below: an artist's impression of the interior c. 1933 from The Skating Times *magazine (ceased publication in 1950s)*

added to their income, and the sessions lasted about fifteen minutes before the ice was returned to general skating. Such an event can scarcely be imagined by modern skaters, but that's how our sport of ice dancing began and grew into the Championships we see on TV today! How sad that these thoroughly enjoyable opportunities to socialise in a safe environment have slowly disappeared over the years. Many lifelong partnerships were forged between the dancers, many of whom subsequently moved to North America and started new lives as professional trainers, teaching new generations of skaters the 'English style' of dancing which went on to sweep the world; some went on to become doyens of our sport, famed internationally for their amazing coaching successes.

As well as coaches, the Westover Ice Rink was responsible for producing many champions. Peggy Tomlin's brother Freddie, a superb figure-skater and British record-holding speed-skater, trained mainly at Streatham, but also skated at Westover with Graham Sharp, against whom he often competed internationally. (Freddie went on to serve as an aircraft rear-gunner, and sadly his plane was shot down during anti-U-boat operations in 1943). Other pre-war notables were the 1936 European Silver Medallists, World Bronze Medallists and six-time British Pairs Skating Champions, Violet and Leslie Cliff; Leslie was also an accomplished pilot who came third in the famous King's Cup Air-race, and co-founder, (with his two brothers), of Bournemouth's ice-hockey club. Cecilia Colledge, six times British National Champion, three times European Champion, 1937 World Ladies Champion and 1936 Olympic Silver Medallist, also skated and gave exhibitions at Westover, although her main training rink was Queens Ice Club in London.

Later luminaries include Junior Pairs Champions Joan Waterhouse and Gordon Holloway, (also Men's Junior Champion), who remarkably won the 1950 British Junior Pairs Championships only weeks after starting to skate together. They were selected to skate in the World Championships a few weeks later, despite never having competed in the British Senior Championship - previously unheard of - and finished eighth, three places ahead of their older compatriots Sybil Cook and Bob Hudson. The 1952 Ladies Junior

Above: my childhood hero,
Graham Sharp
Right: Graham - in white boots!
- with Capt. T.D. Richardson,
(from Skating World, *courtesy*
of Paul Dean)

Above: with my childhood friend, singing star Anita Harris, (left), and May's
daughter Chloe Ronaldson, (right), world champion roller speed skater

Champion, Elaine Skevington, was another Westover skater, as was my childhood friend Anita Harris, destined to top the charts in 1967 with *Just Loving You* and go on to become one of the highest-paid singing stars in show-business.

On the side of the rink overlooking the sea was a waitress service tea lounge where I often sat with Mother, watching Father skate with his friends, until one day in 1937, I suddenly expressed my desire to join in. Father went to the skate shop to enquire whether there were boots available for four-year-old boys, which of course there were not. However, the manager of the shop said he would make me a pair with little snow runners instead of skates; and duly 'booted' I set off round the rink clutching my Teddy Bear (he proved to be my most satisfactory partner ever, since he never disagreed with me, and I have him to this day). Hooked for life, from that day I never looked back!

Music was important in my skating life from the very start, and I would ask the band leader to play the Souza March *Blaze Away* as I skated off with Teddy. (There is an odd coincidence connected with this march. Many, many years later, I was honoured by the Queen with the award of MBE, later upgraded to OBE, and while I stood in line waiting to go before Her Majesty, suddenly the Band of the Grenadier Guards, who were playing softly on a balcony, launched into *Blaze Away*. The hair stood up on the nape of my neck, and I arrived in front of the Queen close to tears. Needless to say, *Blaze Away* remains my favourite tune). These happy adventures on ice lasted until I was six, when most rinks closed to the public for the duration of the war - making ice involved using ammonia, and had a rink received a direct hit from a bomb, the fumes released would have suffocated the population in the immediate area.

Everyone's life changed completely from that moment. Seven decades later, young people can't possibly understand what wartime conditions were like. I rarely had sweets, and never saw a banana until the end of the war! We relied on the radio for all information; rationing of basic commodities like butter, bread, sugar, and other everyday things, was enforced; we had to carry identity cards at all times; and we couldn't go further than thirty miles from home without a permit, partly because fuel was also rationed and in very short supply. I'll never forget standing on the cliffs near our home with my parents as dawn broke on 28th May 1940, watching flotilla after flotilla of 'little ships' leaving on the largest private mission in history: thousands of boats of every conceivable size from pleasure cruisers to small dinghies, covering the Channel as far as the eye could see, setting out with true British grit to rescue our soldiers trapped at Dunkirk. Next day we stood there again and watched them limp back, packed with men living and dead.

Being too old for active service, my father organized an Air Training Corps in addition to joining the Home Guard. As he was in a reserved occupation, we did get extra petrol, but any kind of travel was nonetheless very difficult. Towards the end of the war there was a strong belief that the Germans would win, and things became more difficult still; gardens were turned into vegetable patches, morale was low, and we were all very nervous about a possible invasion. The Cabinet had already realised the most likely place for that to take place would be Poole, where we lived, as it had the largest natural harbour on the south coast - something always at the back of our minds, especially as Father's office was on the quay itself.

We didn't suffer much bomb damage, although one person was killed in the next street to ours during an air-raid. We did however see a lot of enemy aircraft returning to Germany after bombing London, jettisoning any leftover bombs as they flew very low over the coast to avoid our radar. One day I went outside when I heard an aircraft approaching, and as I exited the kitchen door, I looked up and clearly saw the German pilot looking down on me. Quite an experience!

Another unforgettable experience happened in the early hours one morning: a loud-speaker van came through our area saying, "The Germans have landed, everyone to their posts." Father immediately grabbed his gun and left. Terrified, Mother and I retired under the stairs, supposedly the safest place in any house; as a young boy, I imagined German soldiers coming over the fence to kill us all. Instead, as dawn broke, Father returned and told us, to our immense relief, that it was just an emergency drill, held because the war effort seemed to be going so poorly. So, Mother and I could relax; but it had been an extremely frightening episode and shows how seriously the threat of imminent invasion was taken.

In another way we were lucky, because we had American and Canadian troops billeted in the house opposite. Ever-gregarious, Mother collected them together and our small bungalow became their second home. Father, returning after a long working day, would find the military sprawled in every room, drinking tea, playing cards and listening to the radio they'd set up. He wasn't always happy with the situation but bore it with fortitude, the upside being that the troops would bring tea, sweets, and sugar from their own canteen, so we were always well provided for! And in typical Transatlantic fashion they all called me Junior, a nickname that stuck long after they left.

There was no way our soldiers could tell their families where they were, as all letters to another country were censored. To help, Mother hit on a cunning plan: she would write innocuous letters to their parents in North America, mentioning that she had seen Johnny or Peter or whoever, and that they were looking very well. These letters did get through and made the relatives across the Atlantic happy. By an odd quirk of fate, they made us happy, too: the neighbour of a woman who received one of Mother's missives happened to be a well-known journalist, Ruth Abild. When Ruth heard the story, she generously sent us food parcels for the rest of the war, and even offered to take me to live with her family in the USA for safety's sake. (After the war, Ruth published an article about the whole escapade in the American *Reader's Digest*).

Even after they left to fight in Europe, our soldiers kept in touch. A Canadian, Don Jones, would maintain a correspondence with my mother throughout his post-war courtship, marriage, and raising of a family, indeed right up to his death fifty years later; then when Mother died, I kept in touch with his granddaughter, and always telephoned her when I was in Canada for a skating event.

After Victory in Europe was proclaimed on 8th May 1945, shortly after my twelfth birthday, life slowly got back to normal. I attended Ringwood School, relocated to central Bournemouth after the war, and continued social skating while I pursued my studies. Looking back, I realise my education was rather sketchy, but I managed to scrape through my National Certificate and so had some qualification to my name, albeit hardly an 'ology' in anything! Luckily, many years after I left, Ringwood's fees became high enough to qualify it as a Public School - which looks much more impressive on my CV, if only by default.

I remember our school Speech Days at a local theatre being a nightmare. As Chairman of the Governors, Father was seated on the stage with Mother, and had to make a speech. I sank lower in my seat as he performed; he would insist on telling jokes, and comedian he was not! Meanwhile Mother, dressed in her best outfit, would be presented with a bouquet. Since she was not very adept in sitting elegantly, I always reminded her to keep her knees close together and place the flowers across them, but she rarely remembered. I was always so pleased when the event was over!

At twelve, I joined the local Boy Scouts, (whose camp on Brownsea Island in Poole Harbour was founded in 1907 by Robert Baden-Powell), became a Cub Scouts Group Leader in my teens, and remained a Scout until I started Art School. I'll always hail it as an excellent organization which certainly taught me a lot, standing me in good stead when I did my National Service and could hardly understand the Mancunian accents; and by pure coincidence also led to great steps, (so to speak!), in my future career.

Every week, a colleague and I would take our Cub Scouts to Linden Hall Hydro Swimming Pool in nearby Boscombe for swimming lessons. On our various visits I'd noticed a door marked Ballroom Dance Studio and, because I enjoyed dancing enough to organize dances at school, I eventually plucked up the courage to knock on the door.

Returning that evening, I stepped through said door into a new, glamorous world, and met many wonderful, talented people who have stayed in my life. Unbeknown to me, the studio was run by Maisie Harrison and her partner Desmond Ellison, British Champions in both Ballroom and Latin American - in other words, the tops! Instantly hooked, as I have been ever since, I began taking lessons. Maisie was a perfectionist who never accepted second best, an approach I always tried to adopt in the ballroom or on ice. Nearly every week she staged exhibition evenings and invited the very best couples to perform. Her carriage was exemplary, and when I was about to take a medal test, she made me wear a special metal brace that held my shoulders and back in an immovable vice, improving my stance and helping me keep my head in the correct position. In time, I earned the Gold Star medals, the highest available, in both Ballroom Dancing and Latin American, and competed up to county level with my partner, Nina Dyer, both of us having great fun. We were encouraged to travel to London to see the various championships and, because of Maisie's eminence as a dancer, we got to meet and talk to the best dancing couples in the world. Some became personal friends, and in my later judging career, I was glad I could invite them to demonstrate at the seminars I held all over the world.

Also vital to my floor training were Maisie's tap-dancing classes for adults, with a pianist to provide the music - something I believe all skaters would benefit from, because tap brings flexibility to the ankles and it's almost impossible to be out of time! We were also encouraged to create movements on the floor, interpreting the melody, without any warning as to what would be played. This proved invaluable later when we came to create our free dances on the ice, and also helped us lose our inhibitions while performing.

A fellow participant in these classes was my friend Anita Harris. Decades later, Anita was the subject of an episode of Eamonn Andrews' famous show *This Is Your Life*, on which I was asked to appear. TV was still rather rudimentary in 1982, and as I was waiting to step on the stage, I was amused to see that the doors were not operated electrically, but by two men on their knees pulling cords. I walked on stage with a smile already on my face.

The question of what I wanted to do when I left school was easy to answer. Since childhood I'd known I wanted to be a dress designer, having inherited my father's love of art and both parents' passion for clothes. Father fully understood and made only one stipulation: that I train as an art teacher first, so I'd always have a 'real' job to fall back on. I'd been going to night-school at

Teenage pastimes:

Above left: in the garden of Sun Trap, dressed for school cricket
Above right: Ballroom Dancing with my partner Nina Dyer

Left: still enjoying the piano as an adult

Bournemouth College of Art to learn Dress Design throughout my schooling, and my tutor, Dorothy Thick, thought I showed talent. Dorothy, who never married and found her job satisfaction through her pupils, helped me get a bursary, and oversaw my development during my subsequent four years at Art School, so I owe her a great debt of gratitude. (Many years later, when I was appointed Design Director of one of the largest wholesale dress companies in Europe, we had a wonderful dinner together with Dorothy and my parents to celebrate her huge contribution to my success).

My two-year stint of National Service in the Royal Air Force was duly deferred until the end of my course - Fate was already beginning to play a part in my life plan, although I never realised it at the time. I imagined I would complete my art training and emerge as God's gift to the fashion world, having done my bit for my country, and then have a wonderful time in a career I would love. How wrong I was on all counts! Life was about to take a different and more exciting course altogether, and make me the luckiest person in the world…

Chapter 2: A Champion by Mistake

I believe in Fate, but there is no harm in leaning forward so he can see you –
Quentin Crisp

In the summer of 1955, I left college aged twenty-two, with a six-month gap before I had to report for my RAF basic training. I was still living at home, but in the intervening four years had kept up skating as a hobby and passed my Silver Medal in Ice Dance and Inter Silver in Figure Skating (the governing body medal proficiency tests were Preliminary, Bronze, Inter Silver, Silver and Gold). I also skated in ice dance events with my old friend, Faith (Paddy) Silvester, who was soon to get married and move to the USA. Although Paddy and I skated well enough to compete in the Southern Ice Dance Championships, when we competed in the British Ice Dance Championships in Nottingham, we came in a resounding last place! It just shows you should never give up on your dreams.

Figure Skating was not my strongest point. To me, tracing figures on the ice was the equivalent of self-inflicted flagellation without any sexual gratification! But I persevered, gaining second place in a Southern Counties Men's Championship, and it's worth mentioning for those who do not pass their tests first time and therefore become downhearted that I failed tests at all levels in every category I ever entered, from Ice Dancing to Pairs Skating – sometimes more than once!

I was then being trained by Joe Baskin, who'd moved to Bournemouth when Westover Ice Rink reopened after the war. He brought with him young Joan Waterhouse, who later represented Britain in the World Championships with another Bournemouth skater, Gordon Holloway. Joe gave me an excellent grounding in both figure skating and ice dancing, setting me on my path to even higher levels, and his widow Eira remained a friend until she passed away aged a hundred and one; they always helped me at all stages of my life, and I'm enormously grateful to them both.

In those days, when you skated your test, there were only

two or three judges and the standard was high, (I saw John and Jennie Nicks skate some of their tests). Male candidates were required to wear black tights for pair skating tests, and normal trousers and white gloves for an ice dance test. I tended to spread my fingers on my dance partner's back when in dance hold, so as this was a fault, I sewed the fingers of my gloves together. I also wore a holly leaf on a string around my neck, under my shirt, to stop me looking down. The only trouble was on one occasion, when I'd passed, I couldn't get my glove off to shake hands because I'd sewn the fingers together too tightly, and so just shook hands with them on. Very embarrassing!

At the 'zenith' of my solo days I was invited to skate an exhibition at the Wembley Pool ice rink in London. Hockey matches were staged there every Saturday and, in the interval, skaters - many of whom became famous - were invited to skate an exhibition after the ice had been cleaned and everyone had retreated to the bars. Before Zamboni ice cleaners, a team of men would clean the ice to the rousing strains of the resident orchestra and the audience clapping in time, entertaining everyone waiting impatiently for the hockey players to return.

On the night I was to skate, just as the ice was being cleaned, I realised I'd forgotten to bring my black skating trousers - a situation saved by the manager lending me his, and staying in his office half-undressed while I performed my signature Latin American routine. This involved me skating with a pair of bongos in my hands to Rumba and Samba music, ending with a split jump – whereupon I fell on my bongos, scattering the black shot with which they were filled all over the ice. To say this went down like a lead balloon is an understatement. The teams had to come back on the ice and clean the whole surface once more, which took fifteen more minutes and resulted in a very unhappy audience. As no recordings were allowed and one's music had to be orchestrated for a full orchestra, the musicians had to work extra hard too!

Because Westover Ice Rink wasn't full size, to progress to Gold standard I needed to train on a larger rink. Choosing Richmond, south of the River Thames in west London, I travelled there at weekends to be trained by Don Crossthwaite. The idea was that successful or not, I would abandon skating when the time came to enter the Air Force, since I had no ambitions to compete.

Unfortunately, Don became unwell around the time I finished college, and couldn't continue to teach me; but kind soul that he was, he arranged for me to transfer to Queens Ice Club and continue my training with Gladys Hogg, the doyen of international trainers. Miss Hogg (never, never Gladys!) would partner me for the test - a great idea, except that her charges would add to the costs Mother and Father were already bearing for me. Her twenty-minute lesson would cost them £2 10 shillings – roughly equivalent to £25 (€29/$35) today - and I would need two a week! However, my parents very kindly agreed, so I started to go every weekend and thoroughly enjoyed my expensive training sessions.

Then fate struck again. Miss Hogg fell ill too, and in great distress told me that her doctor wouldn't allow her to partner any of her students through their tests. That included my Gold, which required skating eight compulsory dances, plus any necessary re-skates, plus a four-minute free dance routine; only a handful were attempted annually, and always attracted a large audience as the standard was so high. The test could take up to an hour, and Miss Hogg was simply not well enough to partner a potential candidate - although she did have a suggestion to make. Another of her students, June Markham, the daughter of a stage magician from Chester-Le-Street in County Durham, was also about to try for her Gold medal. June, a very accomplished figure skater, had moved to London with her mother specially to train with Miss Hogg – so why didn't she train us together?

June and I duly met, enjoyed each other's company, and agreed to become partners; a little in awe of her accomplishments, her demeanour and confidence on the ice, and her absolute passion to be the best, I felt very lucky indeed. June had a natural ability to perform come what may, always looked immaculate in the skating outfits made by her mother, (who had taken a menial factory job to pay for their keep and for lessons and training), was always ready on time, and always got on well with everybody, which helped me to lose my shyness. To paraphrase the song, 'She Taught Me Everything I Know'!

Miss Hogg kindly said that as there would be an audience for the test and we might be nervous, we should try skating in public beforehand, and arranged for us to enter the Blues Competition at Richmond, the premier competition of the year. "You have no chance of a place," she told us, "but it'll give you confidence."

June disagreed. "We're going to win!" she said as we entered the arena. I told her she was mad – we'd never even met the other competitors, and this was the most important competition of the season. But with June's confidence, and despite my terror, we did unexpectedly scoop first place. That really upset the applecart! Miss Hogg, flushed with our success, suggested we enter the British Ice Dance Championships, due to take place on December 1st in Nottingham, just two weeks before my National Service began. "You have no hope of winning," she said, encouraging as ever, "but it will give you more experience. Skate the Gold Test, then you can go your separate ways."

To my amazement, (but not June's, I might add), we ended up on the podium in second place - thereby catapulting ourselves onto the British Team for the forthcoming European and World Figure Skating Championships.

What a dilemma! In ten days, I was due to report to Cardington for induction into the Royal Air Force; yet in six weeks I was due to travel with the British Team to compete in the European Amateur Ice Dance Championships in Paris, France! The bigwigs at the NSA, (the General Secretary, Roger Drake, the 'Father of Ice Dancing', Reg Wilkie, and the retiring World Ice Dance Champion, Lawrence Demmy), promptly sprang into action; but the only deal they could get was that I would be stationed in Wilmslow in Cheshire for my basic training, so that I could practice nearby at Manchester's Derby Street Ice Palace. I received special permission to keep my skates in camp and to join June at the rink on Sundays, when we would have only that one day to practice on the Club ice at the same time as many others.

With my first champion partner, June Markham:

Left: With Miss Gladys Hogg

Below: With (L – R) Tilo Gutzeit, Joan Haanapel, British Men's Champion Michael Booker, June and me at Queens Ice Club by Ron Duhig, © Ron Duhig

Since I no longer had any civilian clothing, every Sunday I would leave camp in my uniform at 0800, have a wonderful breakfast at the Midland Hotel, then spend the day skating with June and return to camp before curfew – hectic times, but at least we could still practice.

In those days June was the boss, and organized everything over great distance, by telephone, while I was in Manchester. However, the RAF would not tell me, or the NSA, whether they would in fact let me out to compete in Paris in January, or in Garmisch-Partenkirchen, West Germany, the following month. Then came the problem of the team uniform. Mother travelled to London and then went with Miss Hogg to buy it from Lillywhites of Piccadilly; and when permission was granted at literally the very last moment, had to meet me at the Strand Palace Hotel with a suitcase containing my civilian clothes, toiletries and said brand-new outfit of a windcheater and ski pants.

I left the next morning, in a state of great excitement and trepidation, to follow June and our team-mates to France, while Mother returned home with my RAF uniform. This was to be my first flight as well as my first trip abroad, and I had no idea what to expect – I'd never even seen a European Championship, or any international championship before, as there was no coverage of skating on TV in those days. The authorities would only allow me to arrive the day before we were due to compete, and only to stay long enough for the championship podium ceremony, but not the banquet afterwards. Then the whole performance with Mother and the suitcase would be repeated on the return journey through London before I went back to camp.

1955 - 56 was the coldest winter in living memory all over Europe, and in those days International Championships were held out of doors, regardless of conditions. I had never known of a championship being cancelled or postponed through bad weather, and it was not until 1967 that the ISU decreed that all major events and championships must be staged in covered rinks or indoor arenas. If it was a snowstorm, you still skated and hoped that the wind would be behind you as you skated up the rink and again on the way back!

Rain was even worse because costumes got drenched and we just shivered our way through our performances.

(One such memorable occasion occurred while I was training at Richmond Ice Rink, and we made the acquaintance of a lady from an Eastern Bloc country who also skated there. She turned out to be an official of their National Skating Association and kindly asked us, on their behalf, to give an evening exhibition to a large audience, then fly back the following day. Naturally we were happy to accept, and the date was set.

We duly received the official invitation together with the air tickets and details of where we would be accommodated and went to the embassy to receive our visas. There was only one problem: we didn't know that the lady in question had since fallen out with her Federation and, to get her own back, had booked flights for us to arrive far too late to skate the exhibition – at an outside venue where they were expecting over three thousand spectators! Only when we were in the air did we receive a message from the captain explaining the problem, and that although we were going to be very late, our hosts still wanted us to skate and would be waiting to greet us and take us to the stadium.

When we arrived, it was pouring with rain and the drive to the stadium would take at least an hour. As the audience was already seated, we were informed that we'd have to get dressed and put our skates on in the back of the very speedy car! We also discovered that the audience had been sitting in the rain, watching local skaters perform to fill in, and our progress in the air had been announced over the loudspeakers as we passed each major city, then during our final descent and arrival at the airport!

At the stadium we were driven directly to the barrier entrance to the ice and decanted, very travel-weary and creased. A man came up and requested our music case containing the records to which we were going to perform. There was yet another problem: he didn't ask in which order to play them and we had two free dances plus three exhibition numbers in the case! Completely confused, we were bundled onto the ice, but soon warmed by the lovely audience who had been waiting so patiently. Then we stood in the pouring rain waiting for the first notes of music so we would know what we had to perform. They put one after the other on the turntable and the audience clapped throughout each performance, creating a wonderful atmosphere, so we felt we owed it to them to do our very best.

One of our exhibition numbers ended with us sliding on our hips, in unison, holding hands, full length down the centre of the rink. Great fun in the dry, disastrous on ice with three inches of rain on top. Naturally our hands were so cold we let go, and each slid until we were stopped by our respective sides of the barrier. The audience loved it as they thought it was part of the act! Then, with our teeth chattering and drenched to the skin, we tried to leave the ice, but attendants blocked every exit. Very charmingly, they made it obvious that they wanted us to repeat that movement. We had to do three more times. Then they started to put on any music they could find, and we had to make the routine up as we skated!

When we finally got to the hotel and dried off, we were taken to a banquet in our honour. Naturally we had to go, but I think it was two-thirty in the morning before we finally ate. Everyone was so nice and welcoming, but it was an exhibition we never forgot. At least I could wear two pairs of long johns under my outfits, but how sorry I was for my partners and the other girls who were unable to do the same under their flimsy dresses. Skating indoors felt like a real luxury after these experiences!).

In ice dance events, the compulsory dance to be skated was not announced in advance but drawn on site out of eight possibilities. All we could do to prepare ourselves in the practice periods allocated was get accustomed to the size of the stadium, bearing in mind that the skating surface on the day would be curtailed by judges seated on the ice, who would stand up holding their scorecards at the end of each performance.

For the free dances, competitors handed in their music on a brittle vinyl record, and that was the last you saw of it until the end of the event. Nearly every country and entrant skated their routines to organ music played and recorded by the resident organist at the Nottingham Ice Stadium, Douglas Walker. He had cornered the market, and that did not change until we deviated from the norm and skated to orchestral music. If your record got broken beforehand, you had to provide another or be forced to drop out; so I had a wooden carrying case specially made for our records and clutched it throughout the trip, because to lose it would be the end of the championships as far as we were concerned. The same went for boots. They were very expensive, so June and I could only afford one pair each and guarded them with our lives during travel and all through the event. If a skate fell off in the midst of your performance there was no allowance to replace it, and once again you were out!

As for routine, Free Dancing always followed the same pattern, fast dance music, slow dance music, and ending with another fast choice, all in strict dance tempo and very firmly regimented. It was what the judges expected to see, and probably the only kind of free dance they would have been able to mark!

After such nerve-wracking run-ups, competition often came as a relief. The 1956 European Amateur Ice Dance Championships were held indoors at the Palais des Sport in Paris, France from 19th – 21st January, with the compulsory dances, (Fourteen-Step, Westminster Waltz, Paso Doble and Blues), on the Thursday afternoon, and free dances on the Friday evening. June and I made the mistake of skating only three sequences of our Paso Doble instead of four, which cost us some marks but fortunately not enough to put us out of the running. Our best dance was the Blues, as reported by Lawrence Demmy in the *Skating Press*: 'Jones-Markham, I thought, were the only ones to cover the ice correctly, doing a very soft, clean choctaw and good, deep edges,' with the added sting, 'If Mr. Jones could learn to extend his free leg to full extent, next year they could prove world-beaters.'

To our delight – and astonishment, given the mishap – we took the Silver Medal in a clean sweep for Great Britain. Gold went to Paul Thomas and Pamela Weight, following in the footsteps of Jean Westwood and Lawrence Demmy, who had claimed the crown for the previous four years, and Bronze to Barbara Thompson and Gerard Rigby. It felt wonderfully moving and romantic to stand beside our team-mates on the spot-lit podium with snow falling softly, watching the Union Flag being raised and hearing our National

Anthem. It was an experience I'll never forget, especially as without the television coverage we have nowadays, I'd never witnessed the ceremony before my own participation. Little did I know that in coming years I'd have the honour to stand on the European podium five more times, as the winner with two different partners.

Afterwards, down to earth with a bump, I resumed my basic routine at the camp - albeit relegated back to the start because of the time I'd missed. The cold was unrelenting, and recruits were disappearing from their huts at the dead of night. Whether they survived or not we were never told, but ominously, the camp was closed and condemned later that year, and the area it occupied near the railway station is now populated by very expensive houses. The rest of us were trained in marching, use of firearms, general education, and, above all, discipline. I also continued practicing for the World Championships in February, still only permitted to leave camp once a week on Sundays to skate with the ever-patient June. At least I was fit and accustomed to the cold!

Because Figure Skating was not a recognised sport in the RAF, another nail-biting palaver ensued, and it was only forty-eight hours before I was due to depart that permission was granted for me to participate. My long-suffering Mother repeated the trip to the Strand Palace Hotel to bring my suitcase of essentials and exchange uniforms, then I followed the British team over to West Germany, where I had one day to practice before competing in the championships held from 16th – 19th February.

This trip was even more exciting. I'd never seen snow in such abundance before – and we'd never competed out of doors before. It was so cold – twenty degrees below freezing – that there was a doctor in attendance to examine skaters leaving the ice for possible frostbite, and it was snowing quite hard while we competed. However, it was a wonderful experience to skate in the wintry moonlight and under the stars; and even more wonderful to repeat our British podium sweep, with Weight-Thomas again winning the Gold, Thompson-Rigby the Bronze, and June and I the Silver Medal.

Immediately after the award I again left the arena, foregoing the banquet and returned to the UK for the last few months of my training. Having once again missed the best part of a week, I was obliged to start over yet again - *and* my training period was extended! Then when the course finally ended, I was called to the CO's office and allocated a job for the remainder of my National Service. As I hadn't flourished at anything, I was convinced I would end up as a cook. I duly marched in, saluted, and was informed by the CO that I was to become a Personnel Selection Assessor (PSA). I saluted again and marched out, mystified.

Luckily, the recruits waiting outside were able to tell me what it meant: I was going to be a recruiting officer. So, (mercifully), the RAF had lost a cook, and I was sent to Hornchurch Airfield in Essex for an eight-week training course in statistics. I discovered that I'd be joining a privileged group of only two or three dozen PSAs throughout the country. I would always remain a member of the RAF and, even after I was officially demobbed, would be required to keep my uniform; then should war be declared, I'd have to report immediately to the nearest RAF depot to induct volunteers into the service.

I was still allowed out only occasionally, and only in uniform, with special permission to skate at Queens Ice Club with June and Miss Hogg. My weekly treat was to go to Lyons Corner House at Marble Arch and enjoy a Welsh Rarebit, (a posh version of cheese on toast), with a cup of tea - all I could afford - listen to the orchestra, and dream about the free ice-dance routines I would create in the future.

Despite being awful at maths, I somehow managed to learn the necessary logarithms etc to qualify as a statistician, and at the end of my service career to work at the Air Ministry. From Hornchurch I was appointed to the RAF recruiting office above East Croydon Station in south London, and allowed to live out, (I opted for a bed-sitter in Bayswater, north central London, ideal for the rink), reporting once a week to Kenley Airfield in Surrey, on the southern edge of Greater London, to collect my pay. This gave me the freedom to practice more, if only in the public evening sessions and Dance Intervals (there was no private practice ice).

I was also trained to act as an invigilator at exams held all over the country for young men wishing to become air crew or join the RAF. Resplendent in an officer-grade barathea version of my lowly uniform - specially issued to make recruits think they'd get the same quality - I was responsible for distributing exam papers, collecting them when complete, and passing them on to the officer in charge. (Looking at the papers, my colleagues and I were amused to find that we were totally incapable of answering a single question on any of them!).

It turned out to be invaluable preparation for what was to come. For instance, during training I had to read prepared scripts which were checked and recorded daily. I was told I had too strong a Dorset accent and that I had to get rid of it; and by the time I left, I sounded like the Queen making her Christmas Day broadcast to the nation, enunciating every word, and breathing between sentences. I also learnt how to enter a room and deal with a basically hostile group of people in order to administer the exams, (very useful when I became an ISU Office Holder decades later!). If I was nervous, I was told to hold my head high and hum something like Colonel Bogie under my breath; always to keep my eyes on the back row and throw my voice towards it, rather than at the front row, and always to look forward, not back, when entering a venue and needing to close a door behind me - in other words, how to control an audience. My goodness, how that training stood me in good stead in various meetings where people were baying for my blood over some trifling matter, or when called upon to make speeches all over the world, appear on television, and speak at official functions.

At the same time, I was in training for the 1957 European and World Championships, hoping that June and I might claim both crowns for the first time. Her built-in confidence was brushing off onto me; we worked well as a team, Miss Hogg worked tirelessly on our behalf, and I was beginning to blossom.

I started work in Croydon early, then afterwards had to rush back to my Bayswater bedsit to change and grab a quick meal before making my way across the road to join June at Queens Ice Club. We had no real chance to put our free dance music on, but we could at least skate in the public dance sessions and practice the compulsory dances.

Once our free dance music was chosen, I kept a 'Dansette' record player beside my bed and went to sleep at night with it playing, so that it got into my soul, and I knew every nuance of the melody. What we would have given for a headset and the music playing as we skated, or to carry an instrument that would immediately replay our movements! Sixty years ago, that was the stuff dreams were made of, not the commonplaces they are today.

The trips to these Championships were made easier by my immediate commanding officer, who asked permission from headquarters for me to go; and by my kind, supportive colleagues, who promised to take on my workload as well their own, so the office wouldn't miss me.

We duly set off for the European Championships, romantically held in Vienna, Austria, from February 14th – 16th, 1957. My costume was something of a departure from the norm, with a suit jacket modelled on my RAF uniform: black, hip length, belted safari-style, well-padded at the shoulders to disguise my rather puny frame, and at the base of the spine to hide my 'sticky-out bum.' Furthermore, having noticed the men's trousers always flapping unattractively about their boots, I took a leaf out of the male ballet dancers' book and held mine in place with a strip of elastic under the boot. The reaction of fuddy-duddy judges was immediate. The sport was going to hell in a handcart and, (only whisper it), there could even be gays taking part in this very masculine sport. Heaven forbid! It was amusing to see that by next year, nearly all the men had copied the elastic under the foot trick, so you can make your own decisions about their suitability to participate or otherwise.

Added to this, television was beginning to follow the sport. My hair was jet black, a nice contrast with June's striking ash-blonde curls, but I realised it made my beard very visible unless I shaved twice a day, so I started to wear Leichner No 9 makeup to conceal the dark shadow. That idea caught on too, and at the following year's events I spotted a sprinkling of other men wearing make-up - common nowadays, but really not the 'done thing' in the Fifties. That made no difference to me, and I always wore it regardless!

All five judges placed us first in the free dance, and unbelievably, Great Britain swept the podium again: June and I took the Gold Medal, Barbara Thompson and Gerard Rigby the Silver, and Catherine Morris and Michael Robinson the Bronze. I shall never forget the experience of skating the Viennese Waltz, (as a compulsory dance), on an outdoor rink in the centre of the city with the stars twinkling above. It must have been quite special because as we left the ice even the imperturbable Miss Hogg was in tears.

Those were the days!

With barely time to recover from the excitement, we faced a gruelling journey to the World Championships ten days later, travelling by turbo-prop aircraft from Heathrow to Iceland via Shannon Airport in Ireland, and thence to America, where we changed planes and flew to Denver, Colorado, changed planes again, and took a very bumpy, uncomfortable flight over the Rocky Mountains to Colorado Springs. The whole process took thirty-two hours, and for days afterwards rooms seemed to sway around us until we got over the jetlag.

Exhausted, we arrived in the foyer of the Broadmoor Hotel, one of the most expensive in the world. The NSA had given me the then-considerable sum of £12, (now roughly £228/€266/$320), towards the fare - the best £12 the Association ever spent! - and the USA Figure Skating Association paid for our food and lodging, thank goodness. It was at that moment I resolved that if ever I was in a position to do something about it, no skater with talent would be prohibited from realising their international potential simply because they couldn't afford it, and that belief has stayed with me ever since. At the Broadmoor we were totally awed by a grandeur unseen in Britain since before the war, including the unbelievable luxury of an escalator in the main entrance hall.

As we slumped in a group, dead tired, a very brash Canadian skater bustled into the room, announced his name, and that he was going to be the next World Champion. The late Michael Robinson, (partner and later husband of Catherine Morris), opened one bleary

Left: With June

Below: As 1957 World Ice Dance Champions, with Geraldine Fenton and William McLachlan (Canada) in second place, and Sharon McKenzie and Bert Wright (USA) in third

eye and said, "And I'm Father Christmas. Now bugger off!"

The Broadmoor rink was a very famous one situated on the other side of the lake in front of the hotel, but, by our standards rather small, especially as the judges would be seated on the ice. However, all competitors were in the same boat, and we just had to deal with it. Again, to our amazed delight, June and I won the Gold Medal, beating Canadians Geraldine Fenton and William McLachlan into second place, and the American duo, Sharon McKenzie and Bert Wright, into third.

For once, I didn't have to miss the Official Banquet, a very glitzy affair to which the ladies wore long dresses and the men evening suits or formal attire. When the orchestra played *Anything Goes*, I turned to June and said, "That's next year's Free Dance sorted," - and it was! We were all given beautiful mementoes of our trip, including complete cowboy outfits; and on the following day, a motorcade through the city and a certificate giving each of us a square foot piece of the Rocky Mountains along with the freedom of the city. To stay in such a grand hotel was the memory of a lifetime, (I even saw film stars Lilian Gish and Agnes Moorhead walking in the gardens together!), although I would be lucky enough to go back there many times in various guises for championships and meetings.

Many years later, my second partner, Doreen Denny, married as her second husband a member of staff there, and she resides in Colorado Springs to this day - so the Broadmoor Hotel will always occupy a very special place in my memory.

Afterwards, as the newly crowned World Ice Dance Champions, June and I were invited to stop off in New York on our way home – a real week to remember. We were taken to the Statue of Liberty and to my amazement, travelled up in the lift inside the monument and stood in the viewing gallery in the diadem, (it was also possible to travel on up the arm to the flaming torch, but this was a little too adventurous for me!). We skated in a Red Cross fund raising event at the outdoor rink in the middle of the city, the Rockefeller Centre, went to the top of the Empire State Building, at the time the tallest building in the world, and to Madison Square Gardens to see the Rockettes perform in a mixture of cinema and stage show. We were also invited to skate at a reception at the very prestigious New York Skating Club, on a rink set high up on a skyscraper. It was a beautiful setting and very elegantly furnished, in the best possible taste. Duly announced as the newly crowned World Champions, we stepped onto the ice - and June promptly fell flat on her face. A uniformed flunky hurried on to remove her skate guards, which she'd forgotten, while she lay on the ice. She then ignominiously scrambled to her feet, collected herself and off we went.

For me the most personally exciting event was when the journalist Ruth Abild, who had been so kind to us during the war and wrote the *Reader's Digest* article about my mother's letters, travelled with her family from their home in Connecticut to meet me in New York. (Their local pastor later came to stay with my parents in Bournemouth, in the home where the American soldiers had spent their spare time, where he could see the house opposite in which they'd been billeted).

Returning to work as World Ice Dance Champion, I was greeted with the news that I'd also been promoted to the dizzy heights of Acting Corporal, so we all went out and celebrated!

Prior to this, I'd never taken a great deal of interest in the skates I wore; I only had one pair of boots, and a fairly cheap pair of skates I wasn't too good at keeping clean or even understanding the radius of, (they were only skates, for goodness' sake!). However, after June and I won our first European and World titles, we were both offered a free pair of skates from John Wilson, the eminent Sheffield skate makers.

After leafing through the catalogue, I requested a pair called 'Silver Flash' simply because they were the most expensive at £11 (£209/€244/$292). These duly arrived, and I took them into the skate shop to have them attached to my boots. From then on, I was buoyed up by the fact that I was wearing the very best skates available worldwide. It wasn't until after we won the next European and World titles that I picked up my boots and skates in the changing room and happened to see the skates were a brand called 'Mercurio'. I

immediately thought I'd picked up the wrong pair, but no; so I went
storming into the skate shop and demanded to know how these
cheap skates (used on the skate hire boots) were on my boots. There
was a very embarrassed reply that they had wondered, when they took
stock, why there had been an extra pair of 'Silver Flash'! So I'd done
all the Championships wearing hire-quality skates, not the very best
expensive ones I thought I'd been wearing – which just goes to
illustrate the power of the mind.

The 1958 European Championships were held at Zimny
Stadium's outdoor rink in Bratislava, Czechoslovakia, from 30th
January – 2nd February. For the first time ever, the event would be
televised in eleven countries via Eurovision; around ninety minutes of
coverage was aired, though the BBC in its wisdom preferred to show
football rather than free dancing.

We were staying in a hotel where no-one spoke English, and
as I couldn't understand a word of the menu except caviar, that's
what I ended up with for three meals a day! I still enjoy it when I can
afford it, as it brings back such happy memories. (By chance, I went
back to Bratislava in 2017 as a retired Honorary Member of the ISU
and watched the event as a VIP in the same venue where we had won
fifty years previously to the day. The rink had now become part of a
very modern sports centre which included the hotel in which I'd
stayed all those years ago. By 2017 everyone spoke English!). In the
Fifties, June's ash-blonde hair had caused great commotion, especially
out on the street, because blondes were then almost unknown in
communist countries and women would, in a very nice way, come up
and stroke her hair and smile, since we couldn't speak each other's
languages.

At that championship all those years ago, the judges
unanimously voted us winners of both the compulsories and free
dance, despite me defying convention again by wearing a coloured
suit. (June, as always, wore a dress made by her mother). Winter
sports correspondent Howard Bass would later remark in his book
This Skating Age, 'The cost of travel and accommodation for two
people from London can be reckoned at well over one hundred

pounds. The sum actually allowed them by the N.S.A. was twenty pounds each. So patriotic Britons must thank the fact that Courtney and June happened to be able to raise sufficient money themselves to pay for the privilege of winning these titles for their country! As their compatriot, I feel like hiding my head in national shame. How humbling, how utterly humiliating!' My contribution was largely raised from my parents, who subsidised my travel costs with their life savings, (and as I participated in eleven international championships, in the end their savings ran out).

As the years progressed, they were increasingly able to follow major events on TV, although sadly, because of the cost, they only saw me skate abroad once: at the Palais de Glace in Paris, defending my World Championship title with June. Our up-tempo routine, with more than two hundred beats to the minute in the first movement, was warmly received, helping us to retain our crown; and as ever, it was a tremendous thrill to watch the Union Jack being raised while our national anthem played, especially knowing that, for what would be the one and only time, Mother and Father were there in the audience, sharing it all.

Unbeknown to me on that night, my future would hold another memorable Paris World Championship in 1989, when the closing banquet was held in one of the most glamorous settings in the world. The six hundred or so guests were greeted at the Paris Opera House with its magnificent staircase lined with young ballet dancers, dressed all in white, one on each step, then escorted on a tour of the building where we saw the fabulous ceiling painted by Marc Chagall. The dining tables were beautifully adorned with flowers, foliage and gleaming tableware, and music played softly in the background while we enjoyed French cuisine at its very best and danced into the early hours - an evening which brought home to me how lucky all of us were to be involved in a sport that gave us such unforgettable experiences. (On a subsequent visit, the championship opening dinner took place in the Conciergerie Prison where Queen Marie Antoinette was held before losing her head on the Guillotine during the French Revolution, an atmospheric evening with all that history surrounding us, and another wonderful occasion for us to remember all our lives).

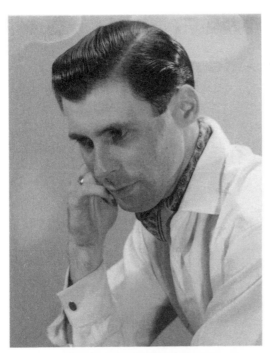

The Way We Were:

Left: Courtney by Roy
Callaway, © Roy
Callaway

Below: Bobby Thompson

Chapter 3: Queens Ice Club, Bayswater, London W2

Skaters are actors on an ice-covered stage

In the early Fifties, International Figure Skating started its renaissance, and the UK immediately took the worldwide lead in coaching. The three major centres in the London area to which budding champions began to flock were Queens Ice Club in Bayswater, opened in 1931, and ruled over by Miss Gladys Hogg; Richmond Ice Rink, founded in 1928 on the banks of the River Thames, where Arnold Gerschwiler reigned supreme; and Streatham Ice Rink, where another Gerschwiler, Jacques, became famous for the success of his pupils.

Over the years I trained at both Richmond and Queens, but my main allegiance rested with Miss Hogg, who trained me and my partners to international success. I believe I actually hold the record for a total of nine Gold World and European medals held by a British Ice Dancer, with two partners - no ice dancer had ever won both titles with different partners before - plus the two Silver medals I won with June. Sadly, we were never able to attempt to win Olympic Gold, as Ice Dancing wasn't accepted into the Olympic movement until 1976, long after we had retired.

Back then we learnt our craft in a completely different way from those who compete today. It was very rare for a budding international not to work for a living. Even at the highest level, my fellow competitors were training as lawyers, doctors, accountants, surgeons, and teachers; then, after achieving world honours, they went back to their chosen profession. There was little or no sponsorship for skaters other than the Bank of Mum and Dad, and unless they turned professional early in their careers, they rarely stayed the course to achieve podium positions - it was just too costly. I know, personally, of many very talented skaters who just fell by the wayside due to the ongoing costs of staying in the race to the top.

Both Richmond Ice Rink and Queens Ice Club were hives of activity, and we were lucky to have successful international skaters around who gave us the impetus to practice endlessly to achieve our goals. Sadly, nowadays this is not the case. Our British skaters don't have the same role models on the ice to look up to and inspire them, and the acknowledged best teachers are no longer in Great Britain but in Europe, North America, Russia and the Far East. And before the teaching fraternity leaps up in defence, just check the championship results in all categories since Torvill and Dean retired from the scene. (Chris and Jayne were able to give up their day jobs, buy their practice ice at Nottingham Ice Centre, and train with other top dancers in the Bavarian Alps at Oberstdorf, Germany, thanks to a generous grant from Nottingham Council). Almost without exception, British skaters have *only* reached the podium in international championships and major international competitions if they have moved to another country to train in a top-class training centre.

The method followed by these successful countries is to select the most talented young skaters, discuss their futures with their parents, then place them immediately with top trainers to fast-track them into a much higher standard without the usual plethora of very expensive tests on the basics. If Britain wants to succeed again, schemes like this, funded by the government, should be the norm; while British Ice Skating, (BIS), as it is now, should utilise successful past skaters in a very public way to help talented newcomers up the ladder, and encourage international competitions to be staged here, so our youngsters can see top skaters in the flesh and not just on screen. Then perhaps with our fifty-odd skating rinks across the UK, hundreds of registered trainers, and sixty-odd thousand regular skaters, we could produce home-grown champions in all figure disciplines again.

Returning to my day, Gladys Hogg attracted pupils from all over the world. Figure skaters, pair skaters and ice dancers were all taught with equal knowledge and authority, and none would have ever dreamed of addressing Miss Hogg as anything other than "Miss Hogg." Her word was law! (We were never permitted to address our teachers other than as Mr, Mrs, or Miss, nor would I have considered doing so. Schoolchildren, I believe, are rarely permitted to address their teachers by their first name, so why not afford your equally qualified skating teacher the same respect, and the dignity of their proper title? It may be old-fashioned, but I believe the familiarity common today contributes to a lack of the same respect and work ethic we had in those days).

Miss Hogg's realm, Queens Ice Club, was built in the basement area of a block of flats in central London and was in fact a club; one had to pay a small fee to join and use the facilities. Because of the shape of the building the ice surface was also unusual - not the normal rectangle but rather long at sixty-seven metres, and comparatively narrow, albeit still an excellent surface to train on.

At the time, (late 1957), I had demobbed from my RAF National Service and was fending for myself in a very small bedsit in Inverness Terrace, opposite the rink. My weekday routine was to rise early, make breakfast, leave for a factory in the West End to work the normal business hours of 8.30 am - 5.30 pm, travel back to Bayswater by underground, do my washing, make a meal, then go to skate in the public skating session. (Miss Hogg was never there at night). We created our routines and practised the Compulsory Dances in the public sessions, and I enjoyed the dance intervals with friends as well as my partners June and later Doreen - in those days it wasn't considered polite to skate with only one girl in the dance intervals. The main evening session finished at 10 pm, whereupon I rushed back over the road to prepare things for the next day's work; or, if we were lucky, (and we weren't always), manager Harry Lauder permitted us a couple of hours practice on used public session ice, free of charge, on the understanding that afterwards I would help the ice cleaner, who stayed especially late, to clean the ice again for the morning session. (After that, competing on clean ice felt like a doddle by comparison!). Then I went back to the bedsit for a few hours' sleep. At weekends, we just used the public sessions for our practice and occasionally had a night off! It was rather an exhausting routine, but there was no alternative if we wanted to compete. The idea of having clean ice to ourselves during the day, or having our music on tap, simply didn't exist - most of our choreography was created 'off ice' before being tried out on the real thing.

Miss Hogg always travelled by rail to attend the events in which we competed in Europe. Unfortunately, because she wouldn't fly under any circumstances, this meant she couldn't be with us when we competed in North America. At first, we found this very difficult, as our fellow competitors appeared to be overrun with a plethora of trainers, choreographers, and hangers-on, whereas we had to learn to cope ourselves. Things do not appear to have changed even today! However, needs must, and after a while we became totally self-sufficient and capable of dealing with any problems that presented themselves, as we had no one else to do it for us.

As well as being a centre for international skaters, Queens Ice Club was also a very fashionable events venue. Hosts would hire the whole place for lavish parties, with musicians playing while guests took to the ice either on skates or in personal sleighs, champion skaters gave exhibitions, and wonderful food and drink was on tap throughout the evening. Some of the most eagerly anticipated parties were those held by the Royal Couturier Hardy Amies (later Sir Hardy Amies). Here I had a personal connection: Hardy Amies' parents lived in Bournemouth, as did my parents, and they met at a function when Mr and Mrs Amies suggested, in view of my training to be a designer, that it would be nice if I were to get in touch with their son.

Naturally I took advantage of this opportunity, and Hardy Amies suggested we meet at the rink as he had recently taken up skating himself. He then invited me to his headquarters in Savile Row and showed me around the beautiful house which was buzzing with workers on every floor and was like a wonderland to me - the very naive student, fresh out of Bournemouth College of Art, who had only recently moved to London. He also took me under his wing, shall we say, (you can make of that what you will), and opened up an entirely new world to me.

Hardy Amies was a most interesting man in so many ways. Before the war he had spent a long period of time in Germany, (selling weighing machines, I believe); and when war was declared and he was commissioned into the Army, he used his fluency in German to become a spy. After the war, he bought and restored a bomb-damaged period house on Savile Row to turn into his HQ; and as he obviously had a flair for design and the arts, he went into the clothing business, becoming an established couturier of the very highest standard and, with Sir Norman Hartnell, dressmaker to the Queen. "A gentleman," he used to say, "should look as if he has just bought his clothes with intelligence, put them on with care, and then forgotten them."

A very tall, elegant man, he was the epitome of everything I was aiming for and the perfect person to look up to and emulate. He began by asking me to help him plan the skating exhibitions at the stylish parties he was about to give at Queens Ice Club. Bobby was there to help me too, and everyone who was anyone was invited: film stars, stage stars, the peerage and nobility - quite literally star-studded occasions, and very exciting. I also accompanied him to various dinners, and occasions like the opera, and learnt so much from him - what clothes to wear, what knives and forks to use - he basically 'taught me everything I know'! I will always be grateful for his interest and the knowledge he imparted; the kind of lifestyle I saw when I was in his company was so far removed from my own.

Another fond memory of Queens Ice Club came about while I was lecturing at the London School of Fashion. (I was also working free-lance from the studio in our London home, making patterns to order and providing fashion advertising drawings for a number of top fashion companies, and providing charts and diagrams for national newspapers for their readers to make fashions at home – as well as forming a company that specialised in making wholesale skating clothes to retail through the shops then based in ice rinks all over the country. Many of the garments were made in the Bournemouth and Poole area, so my parents were able to help with this part and worked with me in a family business we called Skate Ease).

During this hectic period, I was introduced to a top fashion PR named Betty Page, with whom I formed a close bond and who was very helpful in extending my range of clientele – and one idea she came up with was to have a fashion show on ice. The concept was that some of the ski clothes and all the skating clothes, including winter sports accessories from various top-end suppliers, plus some of my own fantasy designs, would be modelled by skaters as well as professional models. The show would be held at midday when the rink was normally closed until the start of the afternoon session, and there would be a buffet upstairs for the guests and press afterwards.

It was easy to find the clothes, the music, the ice, and the food; then came the difficult part! The models would have to be drawn from professional coaches at Queens Ice Club who weren't models, and fashion models who couldn't skate. A toxic mix to say the least! Naturally, all the lady coaches clamoured to be included in such a glamorous event, but unlike land-based models they weren't all svelte enough of figure to wear the smaller sizes provided by the suppliers, (in some cases their only qualification was they were able to skate!). But by dint of choosing the clothes with great care, those allocated to the more buxom ladies didn't look bad if they kept moving, and the slimmer coaches looked fine; they all adored being made up by the specialist make-up artists and having their hair done on site for the show, and they all did their best. Choosing garments for the 'real' models proved an even greater problem because none of them could really skate - they were used to looking beautiful while standing still! As it happened, the few who had skated before didn't do too badly. Others, once dressed and propelled onto the ice, started to flounder and their progress only ended when they hit the barrier at the other end, which did lighten the atmosphere. But everyone took it in good spirit, and we all had a good laugh when we went upstairs to knock back a few glasses of wine.

I've always hoped that this really was the first ever Fashion Show on Ice – as well as being the last, I expect!

Some years ago, Queens Ice Club was changed into an activity and amusement centre. I'm happy to say that it remains a very popular venue to this day; and that Miss Gladys Hogg was awarded an MBE for her lifelong dedication to the sport, when I was proud to accompany her, with her old friend Pauline Borrajo, to the investiture at Buckingham Palace.

Chapter 4: The End of a Partnership and the Amazing Opportunity for a New One

Nothing great was ever achieved without enthusiasm and total dedication

After June and I defended our titles in the 1958 European and World Championships, our paths began to diverge and we agreed, quite amicably, that this would be our last season together, win or lose. Neither of us had the funds to continue; now we wanted to earn a living and get on with life. June had decided to turn professional and teach, while I was going to pursue my chosen career as a dress designer. I really don't think I would have made a successful coach.

On our return from the Championships, we were committed to do a series of farewell exhibitions at rinks all over the country. However, June was offered a teaching position in Canada and needed to start much earlier than planned, so we had to cancel a number of these final appearances. I certainly would never have stood in the way of her future success, sad as the decision was for her to leave so soon.

(Our paths didn't cross again for ten years, by which time she had met and married her husband and had a fruitful professional life coaching in Canada. June later returned to Britain, settled in the West Country and was blessed with six children including Carolyn, my much-loved goddaughter, who has inherited her mother's sense of purpose and fun. June then forged another successful career producing amateur dramatics in local theatres - her father was in the entertainment business, so it's in her blood. Boasting twelve great-grandchildren at the last count, she has successfully founded a dynasty, although none have yet become skaters!).

Suddenly, after two very exciting years being part of a team, I was on my own. Rudderless. It affected me badly and I had a complete mental breakdown. I'd had a succession of non-jobs in the Rag Trade and was beginning to realise that my paper qualifications meant nothing - you had to learn practically, from the bottom up. So that was what I did, enabling me later in life to teach my staff every part of the trade because I'd done it myself. (In the Seventies, as a Lecturer on Fashion Design and Fashion Drawing at the London College of Fashion, I tried to impress on the students that you must learn how to build an engine before you design a Rolls Royce. Not all of them appreciated this and wanted a pass directly into a top job. I knew the feeling - I'd been there and got the tee-shirt!).

After numerous interviews for fashion designer posts, I managed to get a job as a lining cutter in Jaeger's factory off Tottenham Court Road, where I wore a red baize apron for work. When I was demobbed, I'd been given some cash to buy civilian clothes and, (as you would!), had bought a bowler hat and a suit for my interviews to become a brilliant designer. One day, travelling back on the crowded underground, I couldn't understand why people kept looking at me. To my horror - all dressed up like a City worker with a bowler hat and rolled umbrella – I realised I'd forgotten to remove the red apron! You can imagine my embarrassment.

I earned £11 per week, (£209/€244/$292), and when I'd paid for my bedsit, there was very little left over, so after finishing work at 5.30 pm, I did odd sewing jobs to supplement my income. Luckily, the Head Tailor in charge of the factory was great. He realised how unhappy, unfulfilled, and unsuited I was to the job I was doing, and very kindly began to help me learn tailoring. This had never been taught to me at college, but there's a saying in the trade, 'a dressmaker can't make a suit, but a tailor can make anything'. He imparted so much knowledge that I was able to move up in the factory, begin to assist with the designing and to really understand the trade, and I'm greatly indebted to him for transforming my life skills.

Fate then went into action again. Miss Hogg, devastated by my terrible mental state and inability to cope with the change in my life, started to suggest that I begin skating again with another partner. I recoiled from the idea in horror. The show was over, the curtain dropped, the skates put away for good.

Refusing to accept no for an answer, Miss Hogg said she had a seventeen-year-old figure skater who had recently competed in the

Winter Commonwealth Games, and would I try being on the ice with her? The answer was 'No, no, no.' At my lowest ebb, the concept of going on with a new partner, especially a complete newcomer to ice dancing, seemed impossible. But the wily old bird knew that the challenge was just what I needed; so she persisted, and said if she got ice for us at the dead of night, would I try it just to please her?

In the end I agreed. A young lady with a big smile duly turned up, chaperoned by her mother, at about midnight. Miss Hogg, the great trainer she was, knew that as soon as I skated with Doreen Denny, I would appreciate her talent. I grudgingly admitted she was right; but while Doreen was a brilliant figure skater, she didn't know the twelve Compulsory Dances and more importantly, had never even attempted a Free Dance before. Oh, and by the way, it was only six months before the British Ice Dance Championships where my title, held with the now absent June, was due to be defended. No ice dancer had ever returned to win with a new partner before - let alone a figure skater completely new to the discipline!

We talked long and hard. Miss Hogg said that if I would do it, she would support us through it all. It meant that our practice times would mostly be after the rink had closed to the public at ten, and I would be required to help to clean the ice afterwards. Harry Lauder, the manager of Queens, also helped by letting us use this late-night ice regularly. (We got so used to cut up ice that a good surface made dancing seem easy!).

The new regime meant me, (again), leaving for work at seven-thirty am, returning at six, grabbing something to eat, meeting Doreen to skate in the public session and join in the two dance intervals, going home to do my washing, returning to the rink at half-ten - and keeping that up every night of the week for six months. I soon discovered that sleep was not included! Doreen herself worked all day in a dress shop, then her first major task was to learn all twelve compulsory dances - sets of steps laid down as a permanent way in which the rhythm has to be interpreted, together with a diagram and timing of each step, which all competitors must skate - from scratch to Championship standard. No mean feat. Often our late-night practices ended in tears of frustration as I went on and on being a

With Doreen Denny at Queen's Ice Club

hard taskmaster, but being brought up with a sister and brother, she knew how to stand up for herself, and somehow – even now I can't imagine how - she managed the whole thing beautifully.

Doreen's mother Vi was our constant companion. Vi Denny and I didn't always see eye to eye, but she always looked after both of us well and made all Doreen's costumes. Vi was a tremendous character in her own right, a good artist and former rally driver; I admired her immensely, and after we retired and Doreen had married and moved to Switzerland, we used to go to championships and competitions together in the UK and abroad, and I have a number of her paintings as a reminder of her talent in the Arts.

When it came to the Free Dance, my earlier role with June was reversed; now I had to become the Svengali who managed everything and made all the decisions, since Doreen had never been in an Ice Dance Championship and never even met those against whom she was about to compete. Night after night we toiled. Being a solo skater, Doreen had never attempted lifts with a partner either, so she had to learn that as well, and we experienced many falls and tantrums (mine) trying to perfect these necessary moves. As ever, I was trying to push the barriers of creativity forward and wouldn't settle for an easy second best.

As the months passed, we began working as a team and the whole concept started to gel. It was a daunting task for both of us, but Doreen was incredible. She stood it all with fortitude and her customary wonderful humour, and we became devoted to each other, often ending up in gales of laughter. (Knowing how nervous I got, she used to regale me under her breath with saucy stories, even as we competed, to make me smile and relax).

We didn't skate in any competitions prior to the British Ice Dance Championships, so she arrived in Nottingham as a complete unknown, (and was dismissed as such by our critics), to partner me to retain my title. No one believed that even Miss Hogg could have created a brand-new couple in such a short period and hope we'd be placed, much less win. However, win we did - and we were off, cocking a two-finger salute at the lot of them, to win a total of five international titles and a prestigious trophy.

Our next victories against all the odds came in 1959. At the European Championships in Davos, Switzerland, we ruffled some feathers with our matching pale blue costumes, (between my rag trade experience and Vi's skills as a seamstress, we tried to push the envelope in fashion as well as in skating), as well as with the fast tempos and footwork that were becoming a trademark. Then after beating the more established British pair, Catherine Morris and Michael Robinson, into second place, and the French husband-and-wife team Christiane and Jean Paul Guhel into third, it was soon time to head back again to the Broadmoor Hotel, scene of my previous successes, for the World Championships in Colorado Springs, USA.

As I've already mentioned, the ice surface there was small to start with for such a prestigious event, (nowadays rinks may not be below a certain size to be allocated a major championship); and when we arrived for the first practice we were told that, because of the demand for tickets, extra seating was being placed (and had been paid for) at one end of the rink, curtailing the size even more! On top of this the judges would be seated on the long axis of the rink, leaving a miniscule area for us to skate on.

It had been a very long – over thirty hours – and tiring journey, and I'd had enough. Showing what confidence, (or big-headedness! Moi?), I'd gained in two years, I stormed into the office and demanded that the extra public seats be removed from the ice forthwith, or we would not compete. Can you imagine that today? They'd have told us to get back on the plane! Instead, they were cowed into submission, the seats duly removed, (where did they put them? No idea, and I didn't care!), and we managed to win Gold against strong competition from the 'home teams,' Americans Andree Anderson and Donald Jacoby, who took the Silver Medal, and Canadians Geraldine Fenton and William McLachlan, who took the Bronze. We were subsequently awarded the coveted Vandervell Trophy by the NSA, emulating a feat I'd achieved with June in 1958; and to round things off nicely, shortly after our return Doreen took and passed her NSA Gold Ice Dance test. British Pathé even made a short film about us which aired in cinemas!

Above: Doreen and I win the 1959 European Championships, with British friends Catherine Morris (aka Kay Robinson) and Michael Robinson in second place, and French couple Christianne and Jean Paul Guhel in third, (courtesy of Elaine Hooper)

Left: With Doreen

Our success continued with a second consecutive win at the British National Championships in 1959, and in February 1960 at the European Championships in Garmisch-Partenkirchen, West Germany, where we held onto our title despite the pouring rain.

Shortly afterwards we headed out to British Columbia to defend our World crown in Vancouver, where the rest of the British team would join us after competing in the 1960 Winter Olympics at Squaw Valley, California. It would prove to be a memorable trip for all the wrong reasons and, unbeknown to us at the time, the last World Championship we'd ever take part in.

To begin with, as we departed from Heathrow Airport it became obvious that Doreen was very unwell. During the long, trying journey she got progressively worse, and on arriving at the hotel, went straight to bed to be looked after by the other girls in the British Ice Dance team. (There was no team doctor in those far-off days).

By then we were quite well known, and our closest rivals William McLachlan and Virginia Thompson were from Canada - so naturally, there was a great deal of press speculation that they were going to snatch the title from the Brits! Doreen was too ill to attend the first press conference, so I explained that she was resting, being very tired by our long trip. It got me through, but when the first official practice time arrived and I was at the rink without a partner, reporters kept asking where she was. I practiced on my own, checking the music etc, and smiling as though nothing was wrong while I fended off their questions.

Meanwhile the local doctor who was treating Doreen said he could give her 'something,' (don't ask), that would keep her going for a few hours. So, for the next practice the girls helped her out of bed, did her hair and make-up, and she gamely accompanied me to the rink. She answered the press questions about her tiredness, and we managed to practice to a standard that didn't raise suspicions, then it was straight back to bed – a performance we repeated for the next practices with the help of all our female British team-mates. However, we were still worried whether she could skate the actual first part of the Championships without collapsing, and it's an enormous credit to Doreen's sheer determination that we not only got through but ended in first place; but she really was very unwell. and terribly worried that her health would be irreparably damaged.

Free Dance day dawned with Doreen still very poorly but determined to compete. As the stadium was at least a thirty-minute drive from the hotel and we would be travelling at peak time, we hatched a plot to avoid delays with the press: the girls would help Doreen get ready early, and we would leave privately for the rink so she could rest before the first warm-up period on the ice.

The hotel was a very tall building and the lift at ground level opened straight onto a very smart area where teas and refreshments were served. Doreen, duly dressed by the girls and accompanied by me carrying all the things she needed, was clutching a rubber hot water bottle under her coat to keep her warm. As we proceeded through the posh café smiling at fans and trying to look at ease, she lost her grip and to my surprise it plopped out onto the floor in front of everyone - hardly an auspicious star exit!

Arriving at the stadium with lots of time to spare, we both went off to our dressing rooms to rest and relax. I decided to get changed into my skating outfit and settle down with a drink for a while; but to my horror, when I reached down for my boots and skates *they were not there*. In the rush to prepare Doreen and check she had everything, I'd forgotten my own boots and skates – and if there's one thing you *can't* do without in a championship, it's those!

Rushing out in a panic, I told British Judge Len Seagrave what had happened. Then we went to the Referee, Pierette Devine. As a Canadian, with a Canadian couple in second place, I thought her hardly likely to sympathise with my predicament – but she did, and I'll never forget her sportsmanship and kindness as she and Len planned a scheme to cover me while I rushed back for my skates.

The trouble was that immediately following the dance event, Donald Jackson, the World and Canadian Champion, was to open the live TV coverage of the Men's Championship, and since there was no playback or anything like that in those days, timing was all important. So to buy me precious minutes, Pierette and Len, as referee and judge, would walk very slowly to the centre of the ice when the panel were asked to display their marks – after she'd first delayed proceedings by disappearing into the loo until forced to come out by the hammering on her cubicle door!

In the meantime, my taxi took ages to get back to the hotel through the rush-hour traffic. Once there I ran to the lift, back to my room, down again clutching my skates, and into the waiting cab. We joined the crush of vehicles heading for the stadium to watch the event while I struggled to put my boots and skates on in the back. Then we had a crash! The police duly arrived. Luckily, when the taxi driver explained the situation, they escorted us to the stadium, agreeing to do the paperwork later.

Looking at my watch I fell into the depths of despair. I was halfway round the world in a strange country, and by my own foolishness had lost the championship as, by that time, I estimated the warm-up would be over for the final group, our names would have been called then ejected from the event, and the Canadians would win. I hadn't counted on referee Pierette. While the TV people were tearing their hair out because Donald Jackson, the nation's darling, was meant to be on the ice, the British judge had got up slowly from his chair and moved to the centre as if suffering from some terrible affliction. The stadium manager had opened all the doors with instructions that I was to be allowed in immediately I arrived at any of them. Doreen, aware of what had happened, had gone on the ice to warm up on her own; and as I finally dashed in, I saw her across the rink, ashen faced, exiting the ice.

In my very, very crumpled suit I ran around, reaching her with literally moments to spare before we were due to perform.

"Just skate. I'm OK," I muttered, and we stepped onto the ice. We somehow got through the routine, but as we finished, Doreen fainted momentarily. I managed to cover this up as part of the finale.

To our complete amazement, we won! The main TV camera was over the exit from the ice, and as we smiled up at it on our way off the ice, I fainted too, (luckily out of shot).

After the presentation Doreen went back to bed and we stayed on some days for her to recover completely. The next morning, I had a nervous reaction and woke covered in red spots from head to foot. I suppose that wasn't surprising!

To leave this sorry tale on a happier note, a young dancer called Ann Shaw and her partner were representing Canada at these World Championships. Nearly thirty years later, Ann and I became close friends and colleagues as ISU office holders, both serving until our retirement on the ISU Ice Dance Committee. Ann was at the time of her election a very hard- working member of the governing body of the Canadian Association and has given her life, and her undoubted talents, to the cause of figure skating and ice dancing in particular. We have both been honoured for our service by being made Honorary Members of the ISU. Ann continues her work with the Canadian Association; we often reminisce about the happy times we've spent together when we meet at ISU events, and I'm very grateful to her for helping me with facts and figures and making sure that my accounts are correct.

Later that year we were due to defend our British title. I remember, on the late-night ice shortly before we left for the British Championships in Nottingham in November 1960, we were practising our free dance routine at a tempo that would not raise any eyebrows today but, in those days, was *very* extreme. For our final melody, we were going to skate a Paso Doble - shades of Torvill and Dean so many years later! Miss Hogg was not happy with this 'innovation,' but we insisted and were rehearsing it for the last time around midnight when the manager, Harry Lauder, came to watch on the balcony. As we finished - and it wasn't going very well - he shouted down to us, "You made the wrong choice. It'll never work."

The next night we were awarded the first maximum mark of six in the history of ice dancing - and we won. We went on to skate the free dance in the European Championships held in West Berlin, Germany, and once again were awarded the first six ever given in the history of Ice Dance International Championships. It's so satisfying to prove your critics wrong!

Doreen and I had considered retiring before then – she to get married and I to develop my dress design career - but had decided instead to hold out for a farewell season in 1961. (I planned to wear white boots, which would have caused uproar in the competition field even though pre-war male skaters like World Champion Graham Sharp often wore them without it being considered 'feminine'). In January we competed at the European Championships in West Berlin, Germany, an event the Russian team missed because an unusually mild winter had deprived them of enough good quality ice to practice on. To our delight we held onto the title for a third time, sharing the podium with another British couple, Linda Shearman and Michael Phillips, winners of the Bronze Medal, with the Guhels from France taking the Silver.

We should then have gone happily on to our final goal, a third World title in Prague, Czechoslovakia, but for a terrible disaster which brought both the 1961 World Championships and my career in competitive skating to an abrupt and tragic end.

Chapter 5: Goodbye Skates – Hullo World

If you love what you do, you'll never work a day in your life

On 15th February 1961, Sabena Flight 548 from New York City crashed on its approach to Zaventem Airport in Belgium, killing everyone on board and one person on the ground. Among the seventy-two passengers were all eighteen members of the United States figure skating team travelling to compete in Prague, together with sixteen companions including family members, coaches, and skating officials. Fatalities included the nine-times US Ladies' Champion turned coach, Maribel Vinson-Owen, and her two daughters: Laurence, the reigning US Ladies' Champion aged only sixteen, and her twenty-year-old sister Maribel, the reigning US Pairs Champion, both of whom had won gold medals in Colorado Springs just two weeks earlier. Maribel Owen's pairs partner Dudley Richards, (a personal friend of the newly-elected President John F. Kennedy), and the reigning US Men's Champion Bradley Lord were also killed, along with Ice Dance Champions Diane Sherbloom and Larry Pierce, Men's silver medallist Gregory Kelley, Ladies' silver medallist Stephanie Westerfeld, and Ladies' bronze medallist Rhode Lee Michelson.

The entire skating world was left reeling in shock by the magnitude of a loss which changed the course of skating history immediately and for many years to come. America's dominance of our sport was suddenly ended in the most traumatic way possible, leaving a vacuum in top-level skating which forced new American skaters to rise at a very early age, and in top-level coaching which had to be filled by foreign coaches like Carlo Fassi and British former World Pairs Champion John Nicks. Within days, the US Figure Skating Executive Committee responded to the crisis by establishing the 1961 US Figure Skating Memorial Fund to help rebuild the sport by providing financial support to promising young skaters. One of the first of thousands to benefit from it over the years was twelve-year-old Peggy Fleming, whose coach William Kipp had died in the crash, and who went on to win a gold medal at the 1968 Winter Olympics. The disaster also prompted the mandate that no skating team travelling to an international competition would ever be allowed to fly together again.

Doreen and I shared the same sense of shock and devastating bereavement felt round the world - we'd known all those people, many of whom had been very dear friends throughout our skating careers. It was a terrible blow from which we never completely recovered.

However, we'd already agreed that after competing in this last event, (which under the circumstances the ISU naturally voted to cancel), we would retire. My parents' savings had run out, and Doreen was soon to wed the Italian ice dancer, Gianfranco 'Giffe' Canepa, and move with him to Villars-sur-Ollon in Switzerland, where she had been offered a very lucrative teaching contract which included a villa with staff in a beautiful skiing area.

The BBC decided that we were famous enough to deserve a final farewell performance which would be televised at peak time – provided we undertook never to skate together again in any public performance which could possibly be filmed, as the costs of our farewell programme were so prohibitive.

Queens Ice Club was to be the venue for this extravaganza; the BBC would invite ice skating champions from all over the world to perform, and the whole presentation was to be in the hands of the famous producer, Peter Dimmock, with whom we had worked throughout our career. The programme would be introduced by Alan Weeks, 'the voice' of our sport, as he had started to do commentaries at the same time as we came to prominence, and ice skating started to appear on TV regularly. (He had also become a very dear friend).

We were following in the stellar footsteps of the previous four-times World and European Ice Dance Champions, Lawrence Demmy and Jean Westwood. Sadly, they never received the publicity we had, but were the forerunners of the popularity we were enjoying. Because of the lack of television coverage when they were competing, they were not that well known, but just as eminent in our sport. Jean went on to be a top coach in Canada, and Lawrence became an International Referee and then Vice President of the ISU. I would like to place on record how helpful he was in all my various projects both on and off the ice. I always considered him my mentor throughout my Presidency of the NSA, and later when I became a member of the judging fraternity and an International Referee; also, when becoming a member of the ISU Ice Dance Committee and finally, when ending my career with pride as an Honorary Member of the ISU Council.

For our farewell appearance, the Club was specially decorated with the end of the rink curtained, plus additional lighting and seating added throughout. Doreen and I were very flattered that so many international skaters had accepted the invitation to appear, making it possibly the largest ever UK presentation of such a plethora of champions on national TV.

We skated four numbers. The audience was very appreciative of all the champions, and there was a wonderful atmosphere with some flattering speeches. As the evening proceeded, we both became aware of the enormity of the step we were taking after all the fun we'd had together, with so many friends from around the world, during our skating career. Giffe, as an emotional Italian, became more and more tearful - and it was catching!

After taking many curtain calls, Doreen, Giffe and I were left tactfully alone behind the curtains with our arms round each other, unable to stem the tears. We then pulled ourselves together and joined all the others for a wonderful reception in the upstairs lounge attended by many of our friends. For all of us it was the end of one era and the gateway to a new, exciting chapter in our lives.

It was a memorable farewell!

Sometime after her marriage, Doreen invited me to visit her in her new home in the sun and snow. It had been a while since we met and I didn't want to look too pale, so the night before I left, I experimented with the new tanning products that were just appearing on the market. It was a disaster. I arrived with a bright orange face which sent Doreen into hysterics, and I couldn't go out for days! That should have taught me how dangerous it is to be vain (but I never learnt).

Sadly, Doreen and Giffe's marriage didn't last. She later remarried twice, to American husbands, and produced two beautiful daughters, Melanie and Deborah, both spitting images of their mother, and with the same infectious humour and love of life. They went on to have great careers, Melanie, (a State beauty queen) as a university Professor of Music, and Deborah as a Hollywood fashion designer. Meanwhile Doreen is still coaching champions in her hometown of Colorado Springs; we've always kept in touch, and often talk of the great times we enjoyed together.

Chapter 6: You Have To Go Down To Go Up

I miss the circus, but not the clowns

In the months prior to the awful plane crash, I'd been trying very hard to pursue my career in fashion. I now resolved to try even harder. After all, having spent four years at college and with two degrees to my name, what could possibly go wrong? I could sew extremely well, I could cut patterns for all kinds of garments, I could paint and draw, and I had a portfolio of fashion drawings to prove it. I'd written a thesis on Riding Clothes Throughout the Ages and was ready to share all these talents with the fashion world. Surely it would welcome me with open arms?

Strangely enough, it didn't! I managed to get some very lowly jobs for which I was grateful, but none lasted long. In late 1960 I trailed around the fashion houses and even got a job with top couturier Michael of Lachasse: I held the pins while he fitted the famous clients. It only lasted a week, but it was fascinating to see the inside of a great fashion house.

Then I got a post in the workroom of Horrockses, famous for cotton dresses which were popular world-wide, and based in the most beautiful seventeenth century manor house tucked away in London's Hanover Square; they served many famous names including the Queen, Princess Margaret, and the ballerina Margot Fonteyn. The Head Designer, a lady, did all the fittings both at Buckingham Palace and privately. It was a very exciting atmosphere, and I gained a whiff of the world I so desperately wanted to join as she left in a limousine for the Palace or the home of some famous film star or socialite.

Whilst there I watched and listened and helped anybody and everybody in my desperate desire to become proficient. It's amazing how much you can learn by watching – and one thing I did learn was how little I really knew of the trade!

Within a year the firm decided to move to new premises; I

was one of the casualties and once again out of a job, although I was still skating and training in the evenings for the 1961 Championships.

On the move again, I was employed in the West End, at last as an Assistant Designer with a famous wholesale company called Dorville, an upmarket firm that made clothes in its own fabric, 'Dorlinic,' manufactured in the UK, and Italian silks, all dyed in wonderful colours. Their outfits were immensely successful for weddings, race meetings and special occasions, and constantly seen in all the society magazines. The Head Designer, Mrs Olive O'Neill, had immense taste, and allowed me to take a real part when deciding the collections; she was ever after my yardstick as to what was 'good' fashion and what was not, a standard that lasted me throughout my career.

A particularly exciting part of my job was to accompany Mrs. O'Neill and her assistant Eric Howe to France twice a year for the Paris collections. I travelled with them and, while they were ensconced in The George V, I was housed in a side street hotel nearby. If you paid the enormous fee required to attend these shows, you were allowed to buy one or more toiles, (a cotton form of the chosen dress, coat, or suit, kept as a guide to copy and adapt in different fabrics). No-one was allowed to sketch whilst the show was in progress, and there were beady-eyed assistants placed all around the room to make sure no-one did. My bosses would see a style they liked and mutter, "Remember this one," which is what I was there to do: memorise it, tear back to the hotel, and make immediate sketches in my room. Each night, as we finished, I would madly sketch everything I could remember. Then when we got back to London, I cut the patterns so we could use the best ideas, free, in our next collection!

When we attended the Christian Dior show I was most interested to see the actress Elizabeth Taylor enter the salon with her then husband Eddie Fisher, and take her seat in a small balcony overlooking the runway. She had the most amazing azure blue eyes you've ever seen and was so beautiful, living up to all her photographs. On another occasion we were at the Chanel Show, and Coco Chanel herself was in her famous position sitting on the spiral staircase where she was always photographed. She died some years later, so I was very lucky to have seen her in person.

It was an amazing lesson, and I thoroughly enjoyed these trips. Naturally, in my spare time, I also enjoyed Paris and all the shops and fashion. I always remember one evening I was invited by my bosses to join them in the famous bar at their hotel. The challenge came when I was asked what I would like to drink. Not very used to alcohol, I said I would have 'the same.' It turned out to be Campari and orange juice - a drink I 'd never heard of until then, but which immediately became, and remains, my favourite because of all the memories it evokes! I really do enjoy it.

My time at Dorville gave me a very good insight as to how to actually run a fashion company, and I got to know outworkers, to check the work delivered, and all the things they don't teach you at college like getting jobs done on time, calculating Purchase Tax, (or VAT, as it became in 1973), and costing out and pricing the garments.

Although the company knew I skated in my spare time and took my holidays to coincide with the championships, skating wasn't a very visible sport in the early days of TV coverage, nor were its champions well known. I'd just returned from the World Championships when I was told to go to the office. The bosses flung the *Evening News* on the desk with its headline screaming 'Courtney Jones becomes a headliner in USA International Ice Show.' They asked why I hadn't told them I was leaving. Despite my protestations that I knew nothing about the headlines, never had any intention of skating for a living, and that this was a lie, it fell on deaf ears - I was out of a job and out the door! I never did discover how these headlines were concocted, as I really didn't know anything about it.

Once more in the wilderness, for a few months I managed to keep going on the freelance work I'd always done. One such job was for a very famous fashion artist and designer, Barbara Hulanicki, and her husband. As an experiment they had advertised a fashionable tweed skirt in a national newspaper for a very reasonable price, which took off like a rocket. Finding it difficult to produce the number of skirts ordered, they got in touch and asked me to step in, cut the patterns, and find workers to do the actual sewing. Barbara's business subsequently expanded to become the world-famous 'Biba' label, based on London's Kensington High Street, after opening her first small shop nearby - so famous, in fact, that she and her husband took over the entire Barkers store in Kensington with floor after floor of her designs. Even today the name 'Biba' is famous worldwide, and my admiration for her wonderful talents remains undimmed.

(One day when I was at work, Barbara called and asked whether I would like to join her team. I explained that I was very happy where I was but had a young pattern cutter on my team who might suit her purpose. She hired him. His name? Victor Edelstein, who went on to have a stellar career as a designer; one of the dresses he designed for Princess Diana sold at auction, years later, for more than six figures).

Meanwhile my passion for ballroom and ice dancing remained undimmed, and after retirement I continued to skate, if not competitively. Working with my friend Peri Horne, a competitor in the pairs section at the 1952 Winter Olympics, we created the Starlight Waltz and Silver Samba, and performed them for the first time at Queens in 1963. I'm proud to say that both were added to the ISU list of Compulsory Dances – the first additions since Eric van der Weyden and Eva Keats contributed their Westminster Waltz in 1938.

Then realising that I had to find a job, I enrolled in an agency and sat back for the offers to come rolling in. Strangely enough, they didn't! However, I was offered an interview with Clifton Slimline Ltd, one of the largest companies in Europe making outsize clothes for nearly all the mail order catalogues in the UK. I was interviewed by the boss, Mr Alfred Silver, (Mr Silver), and his son Harvey, (Mr Harvey), who was a similar age to myself. They offered me the chance to design and take charge of the large workroom in Oxford Circus, and the money was good. The 'Great Designer' in me was rather appalled at the prospect of being involved with clothes which had no fashion profile at all, were always at the back of the stores, and always very dowdy, just meant to cover large areas of the body as best they could. But with a heavy heart I accepted and began to try and change people's perception of 'Outsize' fashion.

Clifton Slimline was a Jewish company that had grown from a stall selling ties in Petticoat Lane by sheer grind and determination. Harvey had joined the company after leaving school and brought all sorts of new ideas into the production and distribution; he drove a huge American car and had an enviable lifestyle with his wife and family, while Mr Silver kept his hands firmly in control and was a very astute businessman.

It was a busy company and I soon found myself given more and more control and left to employ the staff and help the firm to grow constantly. Harvey and I cooked up endless schemes to publicise the neglected poor relation of the fashion world, and it turned out I'd hit upon a fertile side of the market that had, up until then, been totally ignored. It became a rewarding crusade that taught me so much about my trade, and it was always such a pleasure to see my designs in lots of places worn by these larger ladies. Mr Silver, like his son, was a great practical joker and sometimes at big events, he would go up to a lady wearing one of our dresses, compliment her on her excellent choice, and let her know that his company was responsible. She usually simpered and said how she liked the material and cut. He would inform her that it was washable and made of Coad de L'rap. That pleased her, but just exchange the two capital letters (Load of Crap)! We also organized fashion competitions in magazines to find Outsize Model of the Year, then gave them free outfits and photographed them in elegant surroundings.

(Ten years later I was a director of this company, which had been awarded '*Woman* Magazine Designer of the Year' and was known for its innovative approach to serving a badly neglected market sector).

Working for a Jewish company, I became involved in their family matters, attending Bar'Mizvahs, weddings, and family celebrations, and became very impressed by the Jewish faith and its adherence to hard work and family values. My favourite meal was fish and chips, (hardly a unique Jewish dish), but I got to enjoy Gefilte fish and what I called Lockheim (actually louchheim) soup. Clifton Slimline was like a family for me – I had a Jewish accountant who told me I was more Jewish than he was, even though I had not had my pullover nicked. (His words, not mine!). And it was fun to work there – I remember one morning in the busy workroom when a young Australian lady working there suddenly yelled, "Who's stolen my Durex?" A deadly silence fell. Then we found out that Down Under, Durex was the name of the sticky tape we called Sellotape, and everyone burst into laughter!

We began to take stalls at fashion fairs all over Europe, and as the company grew, I was able to design much more up-to-date outfits in large sizes, and expand my ideas through the major mail order catalogues; their buyers had become friends, and welcomed the increase in sales which resulted from breathing new life into a staid class of fashion. Nowadays, when I see larger size models on the cover of magazines that decades ago would never have entertained the concept, I feel very proud to have been part of that revolution.

Meanwhile I'd continued skating for fun with my friends in the evening public sessions, until one night I had a bad fall. A skater had dropped a key which became embedded in the ice, the heel of my skate caught on it, and I went flat on my back, knocking several vertebrae out of line. Over the next few weeks my back became increasingly painful, walking and standing were uncomfortable, and I was slowly losing the use of my right hand – which made life standing at a high table cutting patterns all day very difficult.

I'd been going to an osteopath for several months, and having acupuncture every morning before work to release my back muscles and allow my body to straighten, but it wasn't getting any better and I was very worried about my ability to continue my job. A top Harley Street chiropractor felt sure that it wouldn't improve and told me frankly that I had to face the possibility of spending life in a wheelchair.

But Mr Silver, who could see my mobility worsening by the day, suggested I went to see someone he knew who 'might help.' I duly went to see the guy in his modest North London apartment, mainly to satisfy my kindly MD rather than in any hope of success. He didn't wear a white coat or look like a specialist, just ordinary in his dress and manner. He ushered me into a minute sitting room and asked me to sit down but didn't ask what was wrong. Then he started discussing football as he moved behind me and placed his hands on my shoulders. After a few minutes they began to feel very warm, almost like two small electric fires. Suddenly he told me that I had a severe back problem, and it was going to take more than one visit to see an improvement. Unconvinced, I made another appointment for the following month, thinking that at least I'd paid lip-service to Mr Silver's concerns, and that would be the end of it.

By then I'd been finding it more and more difficult to get out of bed – I'd resorted to falling onto the floor, getting onto my knees, then finally dragging myself upright - and was so bent I even shaved with the mirror on the floor. But the morning after my visit, I realised I'd got out of bed normally and stood upright – and for the first time in months, I could use the shaving mirror in the bathroom and not on the floor!

My back continued to get better very slowly, and after my second visit to this miracle worker for another dose of the same technique, I was beginning to work without pain again. Much improved, I waited a couple of months before trying to make another appointment, only to learn from the lady who answered the phone that it wouldn't be possible; one of his American clients had offered him £1 million to relocate his incredible healing powers to the United States, which he had accepted, and left!

It was an amazing experience, and I now fully believe in the power of faith healing – the wheelchair was no longer a viable prospect, thank goodness, and I hope never will be. Over the months and years that followed I did have back problems again from time to time, but have been able to function perfectly well; and I'll always be grateful to that gifted man for helping me to live my life unimpaired except for the problems we all get with the passage of time.

Unfortunately, like many business ventures, Clifton Slimline grew too big for its own good. I can only suppose it had expanded without the capital to support so many new ventures, and the mail order businesses ran into trouble with the ever-changing market. There is a Jewish saying, 'Clogs to Clogs in three generations.' It was so true in this case; the rug was being pulled from under my feet and we decided to part company. It was such a sad end to a very, very happy period in my life, and the company only lasted a few more months before it closed altogether.

However, onward and upward and don't look back, new doors *will* open - and they soon did. Michael Sherrard, the famous couturier, got in touch and invited me to become a Lecturer of Fashion Design and Fashion Drawing at the London College of Fashion at Oxford Circus. I remained in that post for some years whilst I also expanded my own freelance business.

One advantage of entering more remunerative full-time employment was that it enabled me to leave my bedsit and move over the road into one of the studio flats above Queens Ice Club. It had one room where the beds came down out of a cupboard on the wall, doubling the floor space during the day, and a small kitchen and bathroom – and after years of living in a bedsit, (I bet the cockroaches missed my company), it felt like luxury personified!

Bobby and I decided at that time to move in together. The rest is history, as they say, and we're still together sixty years later. As both of us had always been very interested in interior design and decoration, we'd always done our best to make our respective bedsits look better while longing for the time we'd be able to put our more ambitious domestic dreams into reality - and immediately started to decorate as if it was the stately home we had in our minds, learning the hard way by doing it all ourselves and making lots of mistakes. Our dear friend Vanessa Riley always said that our homes looked like 'thirty rooms short of a mansion'!

(Speaking of Vanessa reminds me of a funny story she once told me: one day she and some colleagues were at a rink in the early morning, viewing some quite young skaters to assess their ability, offer some general advice, and consider their advancement onto a basic training programme. A young man skated up and stood at the barrier waiting for instructions, so Vanessa told him to show her some jumps. "I don't jump on Thursdays," he replied. Nonplussed, she asked him why not. He explained that he only did jumps on Saturday, spins on Friday, and just steps on Thursday. She leant forward and said, (mild expletive deleted), "Why don't we both pretend today is Saturday, and then you'll be able to jump?" After a moment's careful reflection, he skated off and happily did his jumps. I've often wondered how his career in skating continued, since having to present a full programme on any day of the week is, of course, a necessity!).

The only problem with our new home was that a 'lady of the night,' (and there were many in those days), lived above, and started work each day with a bang around noon, when down came the bed. It continued to go up and bang down throughout the day until, (exhausted?), she closed for business, and it stayed down – requiring us to explain to any guests that the noise from above was just part of a normal day.

We then moved into a larger apartment in the adjoining block, where we could enjoy extra space and were able to entertain more easily. One evening we'd been entertaining two lady skating friends, and as they were preparing to leave, the doorbell rang. A lady in her nightdress fell through the door saying she had just taken an overdose but didn't want to die. Needless to say, our two guests fled, leaving us to deal with the problem!

We called for an ambulance, and she was duly taken away. We said all we knew was that she lived further up the corridor, but we had no idea who she was nor her name. Then we settled down to another drink and went to bed.

At four, the doorbell rang. It was the ambulance crew. They had to return the patient to where they'd picked her up, (and she was incoherent), so they were only doing their job - landing us with a woman doped up to the eyeballs who had just had her stomach pumped, whom we didn't know, in the early hours of the morning! So we laid her on the sofa and called a doctor who lived in the block. He came and said there was nothing he could do except suggest she rested. Then he left. That was a great help.

So we went back to bed and waited for dawn to break, when she told us she was the girlfriend of a very famous British actor and pregnant with his child. He'd told her last night that she was going to be ditched because he was getting married - hence the suicide attempt.

Later that morning we managed to get her back to her own apartment and left her to sleep off the whole experience. We thought that was the end of the saga, but she kept knocking on our door for company. We tried to be sympathetic until the only way we could get the message over was to sit in the dark, turn the TV down low, and pretend we weren't in! But the story has a happy ending, because some months later we saw her in Queensway, pushing a pram and looking radiant. I wonder how the 'famous actor' put that incident in his memoirs!

Some years later we graduated to a flat in Campden Hill Court, Kensington. We really went to town there, and when as sitting tenants, we were offered the opportunity to buy it at a reduced price, we managed to scrape together the money for a mortgage – albeit not for long! Two years later we sold it to Countess Peel, sister-in-law of the comedienne Beatrice Lillie, for double our outlay – so our first attempt at interior design paid off very handsomely.

From there we moved into a flat on Westbourne Terrace in Paddington which Mother declared was 'film star tarty.' We enjoyed living there, although we soon sold it to move across the road into a better flat on the first floor; we put a lot into doing that one up too, and recently saw it in the *Sunday Times* newspaper advertised for sale at £2.5 million – if only we still had it now!

We next lived in Rushton Mews, Notting Hill, some fifty metres from the site of the house, (now razed to the ground), where the notorious murderer John Christie committed his heinous crimes. We both remember it most fondly as the place where Chris and Jayne came to stay with us on many occasions while they were training in London, and the birthplace of the 'Paso Doble' and 'Bolero' routines which brought them such life-changing results.

Our final London home was in Wesley Square, Notting Hill Gate. We were very flattered when it was chosen to appear in the *25 Beautiful Homes* magazine; and to top it all, when we moved to Puerto Banus in Spain, the same magazine sent a photo crew over and featured our brand-new apartment to appear in another edition!

For many years we shared this succession of London homes

At Home:

Left: A favourite portrait
by Kim Cope, © Kim
Cope, reproduced with her
kind permission

Below: In Spain with
Bobby today, courtesy of
Peter Morrissey

with a couple of accidentally acquired lodgers. To explain: for us, no trip to Harrods department store was complete without a visit to the pet department, which in those days was quite extensive. We were frequent visitors, and late one afternoon, having gone in to buy various items including a pair of socks I particularly liked, we found a litter of Silver Point (grey) Siamese kittens.

We were drawn to them even though Bobby, who loved animals, wasn't particularly fond of cats at that time. The assistant asked if we'd like to see one, and, anxious to leave, just opened the cage. One jumped straight out onto my shoulder. I love cats, so I made a fuss of it. It snuggled up. I asked its name. She said, "Charlie," adding that the breeder's name was Hughes.

That did it! One of our dearest friends, Charlie (Charlotte) Hughes, wife of the film director Ken Hughes, kept Siamese cats, and we were always petting them when we were there. Bobby said, "It must be meant." I said, "But you don't like cats." He said, "Well, I'm sold on this one." The assistant said, "We're closing in five minutes. Do you want it or not?"

So we left the store, without the socks and with the kitten, whose price we hadn't previously asked, (very expensive, as they had special pedigrees), and with absolutely no idea how to deal with the little bundle of fluff that had suddenly entered our lives.

Once home, we asked our friend Charlie for help - thus a baking tray ended up as a litter tray, and off we went to buy cat food. The feline Charlie turned out to be the best buy we ever made. On being told it wasn't fair to have only one, Bobby went back to Harrods to choose a companion for my birthday present to make up the numbers. He saw one poor, poorly little Chocolate Point kitten curled up in the corner; bought him, against the store's advice, because he looked so forlorn; and nursed him back to health. Both had very fancy names and pedigrees as long as your arm, but they ended up as 'Charlie' and 'Fred' for the rest of their long lives, Charlie dying at the age of seventeen and Fred following at nineteen; they gave us immeasurable happiness, as I hope we did them.

Cats don't live with you - you live with them, and they're masters of the house. Both ours loved people and parties because they got so much attention, and went mad if they were excluded, or shut away because a visitor didn't like cats. After one New Year's Eve party, we realised Charlie had been going around sticking his paws into the dregs of champagne because next day he was immovable on the sofa, eyes rolling, clearly still blind drunk!

We travelled a lot in those days due to my increasing involvement with national and international skating - I judged my first World Championships at Colorado Springs in 1975 - so we always had someone move into our home to look after them while we were away. Sometimes my father, another animal lover, would travel from Bournemouth to perform this duty; and after one trip, as he was packing to return home, he asked, Victorian as he was, "By the way, have the cats been… um… cough, cough… been done?" I said they had. "Well," he replied, "Charlie does some very strange things to Fred. But he seems to enjoy it, so I never interfered." I suppose it stands to reason that we'd have a pair of gay cats!

This brings me to the subject of 'gay blades,' which sounds like a Hollywood musical and is an expression I couldn't have got away with fifty years ago! But attitudes have changed profoundly over the eight decades in which I've been involved with the beautiful art-form of ice skating.

In the Thirties and Forties, gay men were tolerated but not really accepted; they were 'poofs,' and 'confirmed bachelors,' sniggered at behind their backs; or, to use an Oscar Wilde euphemism, 'earnest' – hence the title of his wonderful play, *The Importance of Being Earnest*. He was just having a joke with his audience.

Artistic professions like ballet, dancing and acting had more liberal attitudes: that was the way 'they' were, what fun they all were, and who cared? But in sport, in principle, gays did not officially exist until figure skating began coming to the fore after the war, and as this was a cross between athletics and dance, it was realised that possibly some of 'them' could be taking part. However, it was like having a death in the family – you didn't mention it and hid behind your fan.

Then with the advent of television, the world changed completely, as did the sport of ice skating; it was realised that you could be successful *and* gay. I suppose I was a late bloomer and didn't really come out until I was working and skating in London and realised that I wasn't the only gay in the skating village; but, even then, one didn't shout it from the rooftops, as some of the older judges would have had fainting fits.

Thankfully, Gladys Hogg told me she had her own motto: "Give me a boy who is fifty per cent gay and fifty per cent talented, and I'll make a champion of him." How lucky was I? My sexuality never made any difference as far as all the super people with whom I skated, competed, and called my family, were concerned; we all supported each other in every way, and in those days, competitive skating was fun. And there were never any embarrassing moments apart, perhaps, from this one:

Soon after I became a member of the ISU Ice Dance Committee, I had attended an event in my official capacity, and afterwards met with colleagues and friends to enjoy an evening meal. Towards the end, going in turn round the table, we started to discuss our favourite desserts and why they were so enjoyable. The conversation was proceeding merrily until it came to my turn to proffer my suggestion, Spotted Dick.

A deathly hush fell as all conversation stopped.

Finally, my friend Ann Shaw plucked up courage to ask what it was, as she'd never heard of it. I explained that it was a steamed pudding with sultanas, served with custard, and a great old favourite in the UK. The tension relaxed into laughter. Of course, Ann asked me to send her the recipe, and tells me she often serves it at dinner parties where it always proves very successful and ends the meal with a laugh when her guests are told the name.

One skater who spearheaded the change in attitudes, becoming an icon for all the skaters who followed him, was John Curry (more of him later). His talent was so formidable that even the most anti-gay judges, of whom there were many in the Seventies, couldn't deny it. By his beauty and mastery of the sport, John changed forever the accepted style of male skaters, indeed the whole face of figure skating, pushing the boundaries of what a skater could do in a competitive routine; and from then on, to be gay and a superb performer on ice was totally acceptable.

Sadly, it wasn't so easy when I began to enter the judging and committee side as an ISU official. Many of the grandees of our sport had been involved with it all their life and hadn't really accepted that in the modern world, everything was changing - and they were very concerned that skating's top brass shouldn't change but adhere to these older values.

Suddenly they found me in their midst, travelling solo, unaccompanied by a wife or girlfriend at official functions, and feeling rather alone. They were kind enough to appreciate that I'd worked my way up through the ranks to be nearly at their level; and being inherently well-mannered, were never impolite, treating me rather as an unusual specimen in the aquarium known as the ISU.

Then as things became easier for gays to come out, Bobby began to accompany me. At first, he wasn't invited to official functions, although given the same hotel and food privileges I enjoyed; and queuing at the buffet lunches and dinners he was, at first, studiously ignored by one or two of the longer serving members. Despite muttering, "Good morning," or similar, they declined to acknowledge his existence. Then he was advised by a dear friend to ignore them in return, and that worked very well. People in power can stand anything except being ignored!

We're both eternally thankful to the then ISU President, Ottavio Cinquanta, an Italian whom Bobby had known since they were both young men. When he went to teach in Italy, Bobby had learnt to speak very passable Italian, and that was his passport. The President never failed to invite him, personally, to any official functions. That kindness, together with the hospitality of his charming wife Maria Luisa, trickled down. Bobby was never again ignored since he had the ear of the President, and we both enjoyed many, many happy times in the company of my fellow office holders at events all over the world. It's interesting that many of the male members are now accompanied by their male partners without any thought being given to this, and everyone is accepted on their own merits. Our trailblazing was a success!

Continuing this theme, it's obvious that sooner or later the ISU will have to capitulate and allow same sex couples to compete in the Pairs Skating and Ice Dance events; so many sports now have to reassess their basic rules and regulations and I doubt whether, as the years progress, ours will have any alternative but to follow suit. It doesn't appeal to me personally, but I'm always in favour of the sport constantly changing and growing – and the concept does open interesting possibilities for a new, untried branch of our beautiful art form.

An SSC, (Same Sex Couple - my invention!), could, in the case of gentlemen competing together, try to present a strong masculine attitude yet still retain a sympathetic musical persona, while two ladies might aim for a softer, more exotic impression. I'm indebted to Elaine Hooper, British Ice Skating's official historian whose knowledge is appreciated all over the world, for pointing out that the idea isn't altogether new; a 'Waltzing Competition' held in 1900 was open to a male/female pair or two ladies dancing together – note, no gentlemen pairs! - and was in fact won by Madge Cave, later Syers, and her sister.

In the modern world, for a Rhythm Dance or Free Dance, male teams might consider a Tango, a dance created in Buenos Aires by two men practicing together to enable them to impress the ladies with their prowess, after which they'd be invited by the men to dance with them to this exciting tempo. Equally, the Fandango was created for two men to dance in a contest of athleticism and dramatic skill. The first dancer sets the rhythm and tempo, then the second picks up and elaborates on the footwork. The whole dance begins slowly, in triple time, with hand clapping, finger snapping and foot stamping, then explodes into a dual during which the partners challenge and tease each other with steps and gestures. Translated onto ice with the movements adapted to a different medium, this could be very exciting

Marching tempi could also be adapted to such a new concept, with trumpets and drums, or even an Irish feel, (made so popular the world over by Michael Flatley). Female pairs might opt for a soft, lyrical interpretation, with the couple creating beautiful 'pictures' with light and shade predominant in their choreography.

In short, Same Sex Couples competing together could add yet another facet to the range of changes constantly being introduced to our sport, and there's no reason why such an innovation wouldn't work nowadays.

Work, both in my fashion career and for the ISU, made for a hectic if enjoyable lifestyle with a good deal of crossover – for instance, I designed the British team's uniforms for the Olympic Games in 1984.

Throughout, Bobby was there, my steadfast rock, helping me to deal with the ever-increasing flood of correspondence and phone-calls, (no emails then, of course). On one particularly frantic morning in 1981, after an endless stream of calls demanding my attention, I was desperate for coffee and a few minutes to gather my thoughts; so I told Bobby that if anyone else rang, he was to say I was busy and that they should call back.

Sure enough, I'd barely sat down with my cup when the phone rang again. I left it for Bobby to answer. His face changed as he listened. Then he began to gesticulate wildly that I should come to the phone myself. "It's Buckingham Palace!" he murmured in disbelief as he handed it over.

Into my stunned ear, a gentleman from the Office of Her Majesty the Queen announced that Her Majesty and the Duke of Edinburgh wished to invite me to luncheon later that month. A quick mental consultation of my not-exactly-packed social diary revealed that I was free to accept; then after being informed that an invitation would follow by post, I collapsed in a heap, hardly believing the call had been real. I didn't think such things happened to 'ordinary people' like me. It took days to sink in, and I kept pinching myself until the formal invitation arrived. Yes, I really *was* going to lunch with the Queen – and I was asked to wear a lounge suit for the occasion.

Funds had been low recently. I only possessed one good suit, now sent post-haste to the cleaners, and my best shoes, well-polished, must suffice to go with it. The invitation added it was possible to take a car into the forecourt and park there; but as I didn't own a car and didn't want to shell out on a cab, I planned to take the Number Twelve bus which stops on the Mall.

I mentioned this to a very dear friend. She was appalled – I couldn't arrive at Buckingham Palace *by bus*! - and immediately offered to drive me, (not least to get a peep inside when she dropped me in the Quadrangle). My heart sank, because she was a very poor driver, and I could easily imagine us ascending the Palace steps in her car - not the entrance I planned! However, not wanting to hurt her feelings, and lacking a good excuse not to, I accepted with due misgivings. They were not misplaced; after showing my invitation and being waved in by the policeman at the Palace gates, to my horror she missed a Guardsman on duty by a hairsbreadth and I could see us both ending up in the Tower before a mouthful was taken!

In my relief to be delivered intact, I almost fell out of the car into the Quadrangle, a serene oasis of silence amid the buzz of London traffic. A gentleman greeted me and escorted me through the famous portico I'd seen so often on TV. I still couldn't really believe I was entering the Palace; the splendour of its gilded interior, deep crimson carpets, beautiful paintings and wonderfully impressive staircase, all lit by glittering golden chandeliers, was completely breath-taking.

I was conducted to a beautiful Drawing Room next to the Dining Room, both overlooking superb gardens which almost make you feel you're in the country rather than in the centre of the capital. (I was lucky enough to get a closer look at the grounds when I attended two Royal Garden parties in later years). There I met six other guests: a famous ballerina, a civil servant from Northern Ireland, a London surgeon, and three others including the Lady-in-Waiting to Her Majesty that day, who happened to be Baroness Fermoy, the grandmother of Princess Diana. A gentleman introduced us to each other, and we chatted over drinks until the announcement came that the Royal Family were on their way!

We formed a line, still holding our drinks, to be presented to Her Majesty, who, wearing a beautiful blue dress and accompanied by the Duke of Edinburgh, arrived in a flurry of Corgis. The royal couple greeted us all graciously, making us feel very welcome. They then chatted to the Ladies and Gentlemen of the Court who were on duty that day, before separating to talk to their luncheon guests. One of the gentlemen discreetly guided each of us in turn to join a conversational group around either the Queen or the Duke, and then, just as skilfully, guided us to the other.

Just before the royal couple were due to lead us into the Dining Room, to my great confusion, one of the Corgis came and sat down on my foot. Although I love dogs, I had no idea of the correct protocol for this situation. Fortunately, at that moment the Queen left her group, saw my predicament, and with her wonderful smile said laughingly, "You're lucky, Mr. Jones - that one normally bites the Guardsmen!"

The meal that followed was very informal, discounting the fact that few of us usually lunches with a uniformed steward to serve us personally, and the conversation flowed easily. Our first course was pigeon pate and the second venison, neither of which I had ever eaten before, and was too nervous to eat much of now; and when I was passed the gravy, I dropped the silver spoon into the gravy boat. Hardly able to fish it out, I airily waved it away - I couldn't think what else to do in such illustrious company. The china and cutlery – luckily, I knew which to use, thanks to Hardy Amies! - were unbelievably magnificent, and during the meal I had to keep pinching myself as to where and with whom I was lunching, and that it wasn't just a dream.

Dessert consisted of fruit, topped by a very crisp biscuit. Terrified of trying to cut it and sending a shard flying straight into the lap of the Queen, who was seated opposite, I was unsure how to proceed. Happily, Her Majesty saved me by rising, thus signifying the end of the meal, and we were all conducted out to leave. I'd wondered if I could surreptitiously keep the printed menu which had been placed on the table in front of each guest but hadn't got the pluck. However, as we left, we were all given one by an attendant as a souvenir, and I still have it today.

The whole operation was impeccably well organized without being obviously so to the guests. Exactly on time the royal party left, we all knew it was time to go, and as we left a fellow guest asked me if I had my car outside. On being told no, he very kindly offered me a lift. I couldn't bring myself to tell him I'd been planning to go home on the bus, so when he asked where to drop me, I thought on my feet. "Oh, I'm popping into Harrods on the way back," I replied, "so that will be fine."

He duly dropped me outside, where I duly caught the bus - I doubt if many people go home by public transport after lunching with the Queen! It had been the thrill of a lifetime and one I will never forget; I was just sad it was over, but I did have the opportunity to meet Her Majesty on several other occasions, so I consider myself extremely lucky.

Another royal day to remember: with Father on our way to a family celebration in Queen's Ice Club after being invested with my OBE

Chapter 7: Dancing Through the Years

Writing one's memoirs is rather like dissecting fish - you keep coming across bones you never knew were there!

British sports on ice officially began life at the Cambridge Guildhall in 1879, and the governing body created to manage them, the National Skating Association of Great Britain, now British Ice Skating, is one of the oldest sports associations in the country.

The NSA was formed primarily to regulate Fens speed skating: when the Fens froze solid and agricultural labourers couldn't work the land, (which didn't happen every year), they took to the ice and competed for valuable prizes, often including meat, to help feed their families while they were unable to earn. Fens skating was a huge spectator sport watched by thousands, among them the landowners, farmers, and even royalty – the Prince of Wales, later King Edward VII, was a great fan and often attended races when at Sandringham. (He also donated a trophy to the championship, and the very handsome silverware awarded to the winners was still competed for until the twentieth century whenever the waters froze hard enough). With so much prestige attached, and so much betting on the races, it became necessary for some formal rules to be laid down, to prevent cheating if nothing else. These Victorian gentlemen thus contributed a great deal to the growth of our sport, which later widened its scope to include figure skating, roller-skating, (speed and figures), and latterly, ice dancing and synchronised skating.

The NSA became one of the founder members of the International Skating Union, founded in Scheveningen, Holland, in 1892. Roller skaters joined their appropriate international body in due course, but remained NSA members until the split came, of which more anon. Its first World Ladies Figure Skating Championships, won by Madge Syers, were held in 1906; her subsequent success in pairs skating with her husband was emulated by another husband and wife team, James and Phyllis Johnson, who claimed the World Champion Pairs Skating title in 1909 and 1912. Other great pre-war NSA World Champions were Cecilia Colledge, (1937), Megan Taylor, (1938 and 1939), and Graham Sharp, (1939); the latter, as Captain Graham Sharp, returned to compete after the war but failed to regain his title. Post-war World Champions include Jeannette Altwegg, CBE, (1951), who also won Olympic Gold for Britain in 1952, only the second such win for a British lady skater; and John and Jenny Nicks, the 1953 World Pairs Skating Champions.

Inducting Jeannette Altwegg into the Figure Skating Hall of Fame in 1993 by Kim Cope, © Kim Cope, reproduced with her kind permission

When the World Ice Dance Championships were inaugurated by the ISU in 1952, British ice dancers came into their own with Lawrence Demmy and Jean Westwood becoming the first ever World Ice Dance Champions, and holding onto the title until their retirement in 1955, (whereupon Pamela Weight and Paul

Thomas stepped into their boots to win in 1956). British pairs including these two couples repeatedly swept the podium at the European Ice Dance Championships from the first event in 1954 until 1956; then from 1957 to 1960, firstly with June Markham and later Doreen Denny as my partners, we continued our run of Great British World Champions and European title holders.

Following our retirement, in 1962 the Czechoslovakian brother and sister team of Pavel Roman and Eva Romanova took over the mantle and won four consecutive world titles. Sadly, Pavel lost his life in a car accident but Eva, who now lives in the UK, is back in touch after more than fifty years, and we're busy catching up! Funnily enough, she too has just published her life story, (in Czech, understandably).

World Ice Dance Champion brother and sister: Pavel Roman and Eva Romanova in Opava, Czechoslovakia, 1963

In 1966 the world title returned to Britain as Diane Towler and Bernard Ford took up the baton and skated with it, bursting onto the championship scene with yet another original style for this ever growing and increasingly popular discipline. Forgoing the usual slow-fast-slow combination of music for the free dance, Diane and Bernard introduced a single melody throughout, building the excitement as it grew ever faster to end with a dramatic crescendo – a forerunner of 'Bolero.' They became famous for their 'Zorba the Greek' Free Dance which broke the current norms with great success. Both Bobby and I were very happy to have been involved with this, and in Diane's own words, 'helping to sort out the music.' Their approach to costuming was also dynamic and innovative. Always perfectly attired both for practice and the main event in outfits made by Diane's mother, they once broke all the boundaries by appearing for a championship in bright orange, and always continued to develop new ideas in skating costume.

Born in London in 1946, Diane grew up in Holland Park and learned to skate at Queens Ice Club at the age of seven. Her first coach was Peri Horne, then Len Liggett, (whose wife Lesley continues to teach at the Gosport Ice Rink), followed by the inimitable Gladys Hogg. At fourteen she teamed up with Bernard, who came from Birmingham and stayed in London to train with Diane, and the following year, skated with him in her first international competition. They entered their first world championships in 1964, finishing in thirteenth place, then went on to win the event for four consecutive years from 1966 - 1969. (Diane told me that Pavel Roman gave her a 'lucky pebble' she always wore in her bra when competing, possibly accounting for all this success). I confess to a personal interest here, as I judged Towler and Ford at every level as they climbed to the top of the podium to become one of the most famous World Ice Dance Champion couples of the twentieth century - until Chris and Jayne pipped us all!

After that they turned professional and skated in many shows all over the world before agreeing that they wanted to follow different paths. Bernard decided to go to Canada, where he's still enjoying a highly successful teaching career, while Diane married Marshall

Green and raised a family of twin girls and seven dogs. Their daughters are our godchildren (Candice is Bobby's and Phillipa is mine), and all the Towler-Greens are still closely connected with skating. Diane continues to teach at Streatham Ice Rink, and Phillipa teaches as well as serving on the management of the sports centre which now incorporates the ice rink. Candice also teaches and is a well-travelled Technical Specialist, serving the ISU in that capacity all over the world. Both are now raising their own families Diane and Bernard were both awarded the MBE in recognition of their services to our sport.

After their retirement, ice dancers from Russia and the Eastern Bloc began to win World and European crowns, the most famous being Ludmila Pakhamova and Alexandr Gorschkov, who won both titles an amazing six times. Krisztina Regoczy and Andras Salley from Hungary, pupils of Betty Callaway MBE, took over the champions' mantle in 1980 until Torvill and Dean's reign commenced in 1981. Meanwhile in British figure skating, John Curry became the NSA's next Olympic gold medallist, followed by Robin Cousins in 1980; and probably most famously, Jayne and Chris in 1984, dancing in front of an audience of millions all over the world – an audience Madge Syers could only have dreamed of, and which established, once again, the pre-eminence of ice-skating as a spectator sport.

Returning to the NSA: it was, to say the least, a bit posh, later gaining the Queen as its Patron, a position Her Majesty holds to this day. Its past Presidents were distinguished members of the upper classes, including a Duke of Devonshire, Viscount Doneraile, Viscount Templewood, Major Kenneth Beaumont, Mr Ronald Gilbey, Leonard Seagrave - and then, to bring things down to earth, yours truly!

An indication of the mindset back then is illustrated by the following tale. Since retiring from competition, thanks to Lawrence Demmy's guidance and encouragement I'd joined the ranks of referees and judges, eventually reaching the standard to be asked to judge at the British Ice Dance Championships in Nottingham. I was working in a factory as a liner-cutter and funds were tight, so I wrote a polite letter to the General Secretary, the late Roger Drake, and asked if my rail fare could be reimbursed. I received a curt letter back saying, 'If you can't afford this sport, don't do it.' That was the catalyst for me to spend many years raising money so that no person who was dedicated to the sport, or active as a competitor or judge, would ever again be dismissed with such a reply.

One such moneymaking venture was the Skaters' Ball, which started in 1966 and was then held annually for more than fifteen years. It came into being one evening during a session at Streatham Ice Rink. In previous years, my friends and I had staged various fundraising dances and get-togethers to provide money for ice- and roller-skaters to cover their travelling expenses and stays at events round the world. They'd been fun to plan and reasonably successful, helping to cover all these costs but never raising the full sum required.

On that evening, a skater came around with a collection box asking everyone for contributions to support a local skater selected to represent Britain at an important event later in the year. A friend of mine who owned a fashionable Soho restaurant happened to be there, and put in a £5 note, (£95/€110/$133 today!). I was very upset that someone unconnected with the sport had to help us fund it, and suddenly decided that since these small events weren't working, we should have the courage to think BIG, and hold a BIG event that made BIG money - but what? A Really Big Ball in a really smart setting might work... but how would we pay the basic costs to run it?

I went home, sat down, and wrote fifty letters, by hand, to fifty rich people connected in any way whatsoever with our sport or whom I knew enjoyed it. I asked them to guarantee £50 each should the project fail and leave us with huge bills; if it succeeded, they wouldn't have to pay that guarantee, just come with their friends and spend lots of money!

Only one declined. So, armed with this financial safety net, we formed committees and booked the Ballroom at the Royal Gardens Hotel in central London. I found someone to sponsor the two best bands in the UK - Victor Silvester and Edmundo Ross - which was a brilliant start. Then, with the help of dozens of friends and colleagues, we found a cabaret artist who would perform for free. The nephew of Eileen Anderson, who worked for Fred Olsen

Shipping, started to design a programme and to sell the advertising space. Her Majesty the Queen, as Patron of the NSA, was invited to send a message (which she did, for this and every subsequent Ball), and graciously agreed to have her photograph in the programme.

Very emboldened by our success, we invited the Mayor of Westminster, pointing out our Royal connections; he accepted, and subsequent Mayors of Westminster attended many of our Balls in the years that followed.

Our first one in 1966 was an outstanding success, raising over £2000 - around £38,000/€44,300/$53,000 today - and every skater competing in events abroad, both on ice and rollers, had their travelling expenses paid in full for their major events for the next year. I felt very proud to have been part of it, although my proudest moment was seeing Mother there, wearing the mink jacket, (an acceptable luxury in those days), I'd been able to buy her thanks to my recent promotion to the board of the company I was working for. I'm also proud that we achieved the same goal every year following, when the Balls were also attended by a special Guest of Honour from the worlds of Ice, Music, the Arts and Sport.

To swell attendance, we invited the British Champion of every discipline within the Association and gave them a free ticket on the understanding that they wore evening dress and arrived with their national trophy gleaming, to be re-presented by the guest of honour. This worked well as they all bought tickets for their relatives to attend the event and see them presented with their own trophy once more. We also agreed that there would no free tickets for any of us organizers.

At our first Skaters' Ball, the silverware displayed in front of the top table amazed everyone. Some silver trophies were waist high, especially the one from the Fen Centre, where the NSA had its roots before moving to London; its members could only race if the fens were iced over, and their trophy had never been on public display before. An impressive sight indeed – never in the history of our sport had these magnificent trophies been seen together in one place. I'm glad I didn't have to clean them all!

All those seated on the top table wore tail suits, and we had a very famous toastmaster in a red tailcoat to take care of formalities and announce the guests on arrival. Naturally, as all the cabaret artists were performing free, we did have a few hitches. A number of budding singers and comedians, acrobatic dancers and formation ballroom dance teams were all taken in the best of spirits – but the lady who sang with a snake over her shoulder emptied all the tables around the floor quicker than someone shouting, "Fire!" Undeterred, she valiantly continued; but when the tables remained empty, she finally gave up and stalked off, to everyone's relief, as they then felt safe to return. (Well, you can't get it right every time, even if it's free!).

Another unforeseen slip-up was when the Mayor of Westminster arrived at a ball some years later. I was in the hotel lobby with my colleagues waiting to greet the mayoral party - at which exact moment, all the lifts failed, As the ballroom was many storeys above, the manager told us we'd have to use the catering lifts at the rear of the hotel. There we all duly trooped, in an orderly line - the faces of the catering staff had to be seen to be believed when we processed through the kitchens led by the toastmaster, followed by the Mayor of Westminster and his wife. We emerged from the kitchen doors into the Ballroom to be greeted by a fanfare - a memorable entrance, to be sure.

One great money-maker at these events was the Tombola, which ran the length of the Ballroom and was packed with gifts donated by skaters, parents, and friends. The real laugh was when Miss Gladys Hogg, MBE, doyen of ice-skating coaches the world over, and a lady of uncertain years, won a chest expander! I think she gave it away. I also got into trouble one year when a very dear friend came storming up clutching her prize. "I gave you this last Christmas," she shouted, "and look – I've just won it back!" Whoops.

My parents and I had a personal laugh when, at the end of one Ball, it was raining, so Father and I went off in search of a taxi, leaving Mother in the foyer of the Dorchester Hotel. Mother by then was in her seventies, and when we got back, we found her helpless with laughter. It transpired that a very well-dressed man had come up and asked her, "Was business good tonight?" My mother thought it was a hoot, but my father was horrified.

Sadly, in 1977, due to business commitments, I had to give up organizing the Ball; and on the evening I presided over my last one, my friends and colleagues presented me with a bronze of John Curry, specially created by the eminent sculptor Tom Merrifield, and engraved with a very kind message. I was extremely touched. It's a gift I treasure to this day, like the memories of what fun it all was.

Meanwhile, I became Chairman of the NSA by a rather strange path. The Association was at that time governed by a Council with members to represent each of the different branches of our sport, (Figure Skating, Pair Skating, Ice Dancing, Speed Skating, Artistic Roller Skating, Artistic Roller Pair Skating, Roller Speed Skating, and English Style Skating); and when I was elected to the Ice Dance Committee, I enjoyed the challenge of trying to make our discipline more prominent within the sport.

This Council consisted of about sixty persons altogether, elected by the membership, with a Chairman elected at the Annual General Meeting - in those days a large affair, held in some prestigious location like the Charterhouse or Law Courts, and typically attended by more than three hundred people.

To follow it one year, some friends and I had organized a barbecue at a venue in Box Hill, Surrey, and we were all looking forward to heading off there straight after the meeting. It was a very hot day and, as I was not involved in the official proceedings, I was wearing shorts and a casual shirt, whereas the 'Top Table' were very formally dressed as befitted the occasion.

I was seated at the back minding my own business when an elderly gentleman, whom I knew fairly well as a member of the Speed Committee, came up and broke some unexpected news: there was to be a 'Palace Coup,' they had no-one to fill what was about to become the vacant Chairman's place, (since the present incumbent was to be ousted), and could they propose me as the replacement? Almost thinking it to be a joke, I agreed. To my amazement, later that afternoon I was elected Chairman of Council, the second most important position in the Association! So I had to walk, dressed in shorts, to take my place at the top table, surrounded by what we would call 'suits' in present-day parlance. There was never a

A prized possession: Tom Merrifield's superb bronze of John Curry in characteristic pose

more surprised Chairman, nor one so unsuitably dressed.

One of my first tasks was to chair at an official complaint procedure made by an eminent Scottish member, Glen Henderson, against the NSA for not allowing Scots to skate under the Scottish national flag. This hearing was held in London's Goldsmiths' Hall; the complainants had hired barristers, as had the NSA, and proceedings took place over two days with numerous witnesses, conducted in an atmosphere of a courtroom. (Glen and his wife were great friends of mine; however, he lost his case). Quite a baptism by fire for me in the chair and I had to learn, very quickly, how to conduct things - not wearing my shorts, by the way!

In later years, when I was elected as a member of the ISU Council, these kinds of experience stood me in good stead because a pleasanter, if no easier, task for Council members was being appointed as the ISU Representative at a major Championship or International event. In the course of the skating year there are many championships, and it isn't feasible for the President to preside over them all; so, at the President's discretion, a member of the Council can be appointed to serve in his place, with all the responsibilities that accompany the position. That means he or she publicly opens and closes the event and is involved with all the podium ceremonies. The timetable and any changes to it are also in the Representative's domain, as is acting as host at all official receptions, dinners etc, and making all the necessary speeches. The Representative also acts in cases of disagreement and any problems with the TV coverage, making it a very interesting and sometimes difficult job.

On one occasion I was acting as the ISU Rep at a major championship in Eastern Europe, and everything was going well until one morning I was woken to be told that the President of a member country competing in the Ladies' event had decided to attend that day and would require sixty seats for his entourage, plus extra security throughout the building.

In consultation with the Organizing Committee, we agreed that a special upstairs area would be set aside for the presidential party. It could only be reached using a very narrow spiral staircase with a small exit onto the entertaining area, which suited the security experts. Food would be laid on, and I was to officially greet the party there before escorting the President downstairs in time to watch his skater perform. So far, so good.

Informed that the President's party had arrived at the airport, at the appropriate time I stationed myself at the top of the staircase. A well-dressed man bounded up. As I muttered, "Welcome, your Excellency," he turned out to be the security guard. He was immediately followed by another. Not knowing what the President looked like, I went through the same rigmarole and was brushed aside again. Then someone tapped my shoulder and said, "The President's here!" He pointed to a man in a tracksuit, using a phone and taking no notice of anyone. Apparently, he had come up in the catering lift.

I went over and tried to say something in welcome but was ignored, so we all started to eat the food and ignore him too. One of his aides told him that his country's skater was about to perform so he walked past me, down the staircase without a word, and took his seat with his entourage.

At the end of the girl's performance and in direct opposition to the rules, he leant over the barrier and presented her with a bouquet the size of Kew Gardens, then turned on his heel and left with all his entourage trailing behind him. I learnt later that he was a most unpopular person in the country where the event was being staged, and there could have been a riot had he stayed. Being the ISU Rep does have some disadvantages!

Another occasion which doesn't have any happy memories took place in 2007. We'd been in Japan attending the Tokyo World Championships together with many judges from Australia who, as always, were great fun to be with. Some of them would, like me, be travelling on to Canada for the World Synchronized Championships; others planned to return home the next day to attend an Australian Association seminar in Sydney, along with some other judges and officials who had officiated in Japan.

The closing banquet on our final night in Tokyo had gone on late into the night. Most of us, already tired, laughingly declined to join our Australian friends in continuing the festivities in a bar at the top of the skyscraper hotel and went to rest before the long flight.

On my arrival in London, Ontario, as usual I was welcomed warmly – I'd spent a lot of time in Canada, had many friends there, and was looking forward to officiating at a Synchronized event for the first time. It involved hundreds of young skaters, all very excited at competing in such a prestigious event, and I was due to officially open it at six-thirty that evening with a speech of welcome to the assembled skaters and officials.

Shortly beforehand I was in my hotel suite sorting out the words when I received the most awful message. After an evening spent celebrating the team's performance at one of the restaurants overlooking Australia's famous Sydney Harbour, many of the people we'd been with in Tokyo some forty-eight hours earlier had decided to take a late-night trip in a friend's boat. In the darkness, in the worst boating accident in the Harbour's history, their small vessel was sliced in half by a harbour steamer as it passed beneath the unlit arch of the bridge. At that moment they were unable to tell me who had died, been injured, or survived; and because of the time difference, no-one except myself even knew yet that the tragedy had happened.

You can imagine my complete shock and disbelief. I was just about to address around six hundred excited skaters. Now I had to tell them some of their most popular friends and compatriots may have been killed or maimed. (We later learned that four people had died, including young Morgan Innes, the 2006 Queensland Intermediate Ladies Champion, and there were two badly injured survivors including Morgan's coach Liz Cain, who lost a leg). I had never then, nor since, been presented with such a terrible dilemma. Even after all these years, I can't remember what I actually said, but the Championships were certainly spoilt for the duration, and synchronized skating took many years to recover. We lost so many dear friends in that dreadful accident, and always wished that we'd accepted their invitation to the bar at the top of the hotel on our last night together in Tokyo.

Another year that shook the skating world and ISU was 2003. On the night of March 21st, British officials including myself flew from Heathrow Airport to attend the forthcoming World Figure

Skating Championships in Washington, DC. Recently elected to the ISU Council, I was on my way with them to attend the Championships as well as various meetings being held during the event. War with Iraq was very close, and there was huge tension across the world – when we left the UK we were at peace, and by the time we landed in the USA, we were at war! Consequently, we were escorted to the Marriot Hotel on Pennsylvania Avenue with armed guards on all the transport, and suddenly realised we were only a very short walk from the White House, therefore lucky to be in the world's best guarded airspace. Helicopters were continually droning overhead and there was a show of military strength all around; it was daunting but exciting to be part of history at such a time. All the buses taking skaters and officials to events and practices at the arena were accompanied by armed guards, and the security in the hotel and throughout the city was unprecedented - like a city under siege.

Within the relatively small world of ice skating, war was also breaking out. After a couple of days, we were told a very special meeting was to be held, to which we were all invited. It transpired that, quite out of the blue, a completely new, international association was threatening to take over the skating world and all its events and Championships. The news had been kept very secret, (apparently all those involved risked a six-figure fine should they leak the plans to the press or public), because it was a very serious threat to the authority of the ISU, which had governed the sport since 1892.

What horrified us most were the names of those threatening the existence of the Union and wanting to completely dominate the sport: coaches, past champions, serving referees and judges, members of the committees - all people who'd been loyal throughout their careers to the present governing body, but now wanted to rip the whole edifice of skating apart and travel a completely different path.

Worse still was the timing of this breakaway Federation, now named as the World Skating Federation. The launch of the WSF had been carefully and professionally planned to make a huge impact on everyone. All the attention previously focused on the skaters was immediately deflected by this unfair bombshell.

We realised that a lot of adverse publicity had been prepared well in advance. When the events were starting it was an accepted courtesy that the President, Ottavio Cinquanta, would be announced at every main session. However, each time he was announced, there was booing from a large section of the audience. The President was very unhappy and embarrassed by this. In the end he leant forward and asked the lady seated in front of him why she was booing him so loudly. "Because I was told to do so," came the reply!

The Council met immediately under the chairmanship of President Cinquanta. Happily, as he himself was a member of the International Olympic Committee, he immediately arranged for the IOC to send a letter stating that, under no circumstances, would another group or federation be permitted to replace the present member - which meant that the newly proposed Federation would be ineligible to send skaters to any future Winter Olympic Games.

Thanks to this intervention, the whole plan disintegrated. However, the atmosphere of the World Championships was ruined, and we all felt very sorry that what should have been a wonderful event for the skaters was overshadowed by the machinations of a few ambitious people who were obviously very well backed financially.

Soon after the Championships finished, the ISU began a series of legal cases to disbar those who had rebelled from ever being part of the organization again. Naturally these members countersued. There followed many months of court cases both in the United States and in Switzerland, where the ISU has its headquarters, and I'm happy that the ISU succeeded in winning every one of them!

Those concerned were requested, in due course, to attend meetings of the Council in Lausanne where they were accompanied by their legal advisors, as was the Council, and the cases for their removal from the list of members would be considered. For me, as a new member, this was very harrowing. All of those pleading their cases had been a huge part of my life for fifty years. I knew them all very well as judges, referees, and officials at nearly every event I'd ever attended or participated in - and now I had to sit in judgement as to whether they should continue to be members, or be cast out ignominiously as traitors to our Union.

The aftermath of their foolhardy behaviour was very sad. Old friends became embittered that some had been part of this new venture, and friendships were ended forever. It caused a great deal of unhappiness, and I personally lost friends I'd known nearly all my skating life. It took years for these wounds to heal. However, I'm happy to say that in three cases, these friendships have been renewed and our differences forgotten; and the outcome of the whole sorry saga was that the ISU ended up stronger and more determined than ever to do its best for skaters in every discipline - as it remains to this day, and has an enviable reputation throughout the world.

A happier memory of those Championships was the wonderful dinner given by our hosts, the USFSA, in the White House Conservatory. One of the USA judges was a retired military man who had been the musician in charge of the White House Military Band, and arranged for them to play throughout the dinner, all dressed in their uniforms. The music was fantastic and the atmosphere unforgettable, with the musicians playing and moving around the tables and everyone joining in.

So ended an event memorable in more ways than one!

After chairing the Association for some years, I became President when Leonard Seagrave, OBE, sadly died in 1984 after a very impressive presidency that included hosting Her Majesty the Queen, as Patron of the NSA, and the Duke of Edinburgh at the Association's Centenary Gala in Wembley Stadium in March 1979.

In those days there was only a small paid staff in the London office, and normally events were organized in a rather haphazard manner using amateur volunteers, but the good thing was that it worked, and we all enjoyed our events. An organizing committee was usually formed for specific events, with a Treasurer and a Chair appointed to oversee the event in its entirety; we all gave our time and enthusiasm freely, and many of the friendships we formed during our committee meetings last to this day.

In 1979, the President asked me, as Chairman of the Council, to help form a committee from both the ice and roller skaters to arrange the whole evening, during which Her Majesty would present a commemorative medal to all Olympic and World Champions present from the ice and roller world, and then skaters from all over the world would be invited to take part in a Gala performance. The BBC agreed to televise the whole event, all the arrangements were in hand, and on the day of the Gala we stayed in a hotel a short walk from the stadium, together with all the past champions who had agreed to attend.

Rehearsals started early in the morning, and with so many champion egos to cope with, soon degenerated into fixing the order of skating and other small but very irritating problems. The BBC had terrible trouble deciding who should skate last: John Curry as our most recent Olympian, or Robin Cousins as our reigning British Champion. I was brought into the row until we eventually reached the compromise that one would skate last on the evening and the other on the televised version for later transmission.

It had been a very trying afternoon, and I suddenly realised that I would be late unless I went to put my dinner suit on and mentally prepare for the important evening ahead. I duly rushed back to the hotel, and while I was changing, something struck me. A half dozen or so ambassadors would be attending from countries represented by the skaters. I'd had a list of their names, which I'd practised pronouncing – but I had no idea what they looked like.

Consequently, I found myself standing in the vast concourse of Wembley Stadium trying to think how to pick out the ambassadors from the general public. This was a dilemma. Then I spied a very handsome, important-looking gentleman standing nearby, and plucked up the courage to ask him if *he* was an ambassador.

He smiled broadly. Yes indeed, he was the United States Ambassador. Bingo! I'd scored a winner. I explained my problem. He, very charmingly, said he knew them all and would stay with me and point them out as they arrived. True to his word, he did this, enabling me to greet each ambassador personally and conduct them to the receiving line. The US Ambassador really saved my life that night.

It had been arranged that when the Royal Party arrived, they would be welcomed by the President and myself together with other dignitaries from the Council; Leonard Seagrave would introduce them to the Queen, and I would follow to introduce them to the Duke of

Edinburgh. Everything was going well until, introducing a British International Referee to Prince Philip, after all those ambassadors my mind simply went blank. Luckily, she stepped forward and introduced herself, (Mollie Phillips – never a shrinking violet), and I was saved.

We went on to have a splendid evening, and I still have the souvenir programme you could buy for 50p (about £2.50/€2.9/$3.49 today)! For such a grand occasion, the music throughout was performed by the bands of the Blues & Royals, Horse Guards, First Dragoon Guards, and their trumpeters. The first performance was a demonstration of English Style Skating, (the original form of organized figure skating with partners, seldom before seen in public), by the Royal Skating Club (Richmond) and the Southampton Ice Dance and Figure Skating Club, and went on to feature a host of world stars: Lisa Marie Allen, USA; Tai Babilonia and Randy Gardener, USA; Sabine Baesz and Tassilo Thierbach, DDR; Denise Biellmann, Switzerland; Robin Cousins, GB; John Curry, GB; Marina Chourasia and Sergei Shakrai, USSR; John Curry, GB; Linda Fratianne, USA; Jan Hoffman, DDR; Flaimir Kovalev, USSR; Natalia Linnichuk and Gennadi Karponosov, USSR; Irina Moiseeva and Andrei Minenkov, USSR; Krisztina Regoczy and Andras Sallay, Hungary; Charles Tickner, USA; and Emi Watanabe, Japan.

Once in the Royal Box, proceedings began well and the standard of skating was, naturally, world class. The Queen and Duke chatted to me and the President throughout the performances – both are so easy to entertain and interesting to talk to. Then came the interval. The royal couple were escorted to the receiving room, where snacks had been prepared. Of course, no-one could start to eat until royalty did, so we all stood round eyeing the repast, absolutely starving after such a long day. As soon as the Queen picked up something to eat, it was like a plague of locusts descending.

After the interval, twenty-six past and current World Champions, both on ice and rollers, duly stepped forth to receive their specially designed commemorative medals. I was very lucky to receive two – one with each of my two partners – which caused rather a droll situation, because I was standing beside Her Majesty and introducing the skaters to her. Accordingly, when June

Markham's name was called, I went to join her for the presentation, then returned to duty, repeating the process when Doreen Denny was announced. This appeared to amuse the Queen immensely.

The Centenary Gala took a great deal of preparation but was absolutely worthwhile and remains to this day a wonderful memory. Alas, if the occasion is repeated in 2079, I will not be available!

(Another funny incident I recall from a major event in these days was when it *wasn't* 'alright on the night,'.

At the time, national championships were sponsored by various large companies, and on this occasion, the sponsors were a worldwide drinks company based in Scandinavia. On the evening of the finals, one of my responsibilities was to host the Chairman and his wife, and then when the time came, to escort said wife, (a very charming lady, but rather shy and reserved), down to present the trophies, which were arrayed on a table on the ice with a carpet leading to it.

Unfortunately, whoever laid the carpet had forgotten to water underneath to make it freeze and stick. We duly arrived at the barrier entrance. I stepped forward and took the lady's hand to introduce her onto the carpet ahead of me; and as she stepped on, it began to move. She, with one foot on dry land, very slowly began to do the splits, still holding my hand. I had no idea what to do. I felt I could hardly grab her round the waist and haul her up, so she continued her downward slide, (I was not gentleman enough to join her!), until one of the attendants took pity on us and pulled her upright once more.

By then, you can imagine the audience were in fits, and the poor lady puce with embarrassment as she made the presentations. Apparently, it became one of the most famous 'out-takes' of all time, constantly shown on the popular ITV programme *It'll Be Alright On The Night* and a cult special in similar TV shows in her home country and all over Europe. Probably the poor lady never got over her night, almost literally, on the ice!).

Speaking of TV programmes: I was rather surprised and

flattered to be approached by the producer of the BBC's popular long-running quiz show, *MasterMind*, which features all sorts of contestants and topics, and asked if I could prepare one hundred and fifty questions on the sport of figure skating because one contestant had chosen this as his first-round specialist subject. All became clear when I discovered his name: Dennis Bird, my very good, (and now, sadly, late), friend and the NSA's official historian.

I had to prepare the questions in three groups: fifty easy ones, fifty of medium difficulty, and fifty hard ones. Strangely, I found it more difficult than I'd imagined, but duly submitted them and they were used in the show. (Dennis never knew that I'd composed them, and unfortunately didn't score a high enough mark to move forward to the next round).

Quite some time later, after I'd stepped down from my position in the Association and Dennis had passed away, his widow offered his very valuable collection of ice skating artefacts, archival material - including the minutes of the first meeting of the founding Fen centre, reputedly worth £10,000 – and valuable first editions of skating books from all over the world, amassed over a lifetime, to the NSA for safe-keeping.

I got to hear that the Association had turned this offer down, the then Chief Executive even making the outrageous suggestion that they should be thrown away! Luckily, I'd been collaborating with Professor James Hines, PhD, of the Christopher Newport University in Virginia, USA, with the preparation of his brilliant *History of Figure Skating*, so I asked him if he'd be interested in taking these historical items into the University Library. He immediately agreed. Flying over at once to visit Mrs Bird, he chose dozens of Dennis's books and pieces of memorabilia and had them shipped over to the States where they have remained ever since. How sad that our own national association should have chosen to deprive British authors seeking reference of a collection of irreplaceable books, papers and photos covering two hundred years of world skating! A younger generation might well have found it a history worth remembering.

Chapter 8: Raising the Ice Curtain

From Russia with love

Looking back on the names on that 1979 NSA Centenary Programme, it seems incredible that when Doreen and I retired in 1961, there were no entries from Russia at all in the European Championships, let alone the World Championships. Russia's eminence in ice dancing today, together with the figure skating successes of its countrymen and women, illustrate how much things have changed and how barriers between competing nations have dropped; the amazing camaraderie that exists between all skaters of every age and standard makes our skating world what it now is.

When Russian skaters began to compete, they lacked equipment and boots of the necessary quality - deficiencies which soon disappeared as the State took charge. Coaches, now allowed to travel with their skaters, (albeit closely monitored by team leaders throughout the event), watched, listened and learnt. To a certain extent, ice dancing then followed the same path John Curry had forged in figure skating: Liudmila Pakhomova and Alexandr Gorshkov introduced very musical, exciting routines, using choreography and speed over the ice such as had never been seen before - techniques soon emulated by other couples all over the world, using new ideas and movements to create a truly 'Free' Dance which became one of the highlights of any competition or Championship. The same could be said of pairs skating, an art form at which the Russians excelled, and again led the way with new ideas.

In 1958, the first Russian ice dance couple to skate in the European Championships were Svetlana Smirnova and Leonid Gordon, who came last; the second were Nadezhda Velle and Alexander Treshchev, who claimed thirteenth place in 1965. In 1966, Viktor Ryzhkin appeared with a new partner, the unknown Liudmila Pakhomova, (whom he had initially coached), and reached seventh place in the Europeans and tenth in the World Championships. By 1967, both had changed partners, and Liudmila was skating with

Alexandr Gorshkov; Ryzhkin claimed fourth place with Irina Grishkova, beating Liudmila and Alexandr into fifth at the Europeans, while at the World Championships, Grishkova and Ryzhkin came seventh, ahead of Pakhomova and Gorshkov in thirteenth place. In 1968, the latter achieved fifth place, one below their fellow Russians in the Europeans, and sixth in the World Championships, again one place below their compatriots. Incredibly, by 1969 they had reached the podium, taking a Bronze Medal at the European Championships and a Silver in the World Championships – and in 1970, they became European and World Champions, beginning their collection of titles unequalled to this day. The couple went on to win the European Ice Dance title again in 1971; took Silver in 1972; then regained and held onto their crown from 1973 - 1976. They were also World Champions from 1970 – 1974, but didn't compete in 1975 due to illness, (their compatriots Irina Moiseeva and Andrei Minenkov won that year). However, in 1976 they were fit to reclaim their World title and, their crowning glory, to win the coveted first-ever Olympic Gold Ice Dance Medal, prior to retiring as the most decorated ice dancers of all time. After Liudmila's untimely death in 1986 from leukaemia at the age of thirty-nine, she was mourned throughout Russia, commemorated on a stamp, and had a minor planet named after her. Two years later, she and Alexandr were inducted into the World Figure Skating Hall of Fame, and in 2010, he received the honour of a unanimous election to the Presidency of the Russian Figure Skating Federation. I'm honoured to have been their friend, and to have served under Alexandr's chairmanship of the ISU Ice Dance Committee.

Years later, when I was judging an international competition, I congratulated Liudmila and Alexandr, (who by then were married), on their achievements; and at the post-competition party, a very famous Russian pair skating coach, Alexandr Zhuk, said that Russian ice dancing owed much to the videos of Doreen and myself during our competitive career to teach their own ice dancers how to compete, now with increasing success, against the rest of the world. Quite an accolade! However, I honestly believe that Russians are born with music in their soul. Unlike many other countries, Russia introduces children to music and dancing at the earliest age through their national dances. Ballet is intrinsic to their childhood, and not considered feminine – quite the opposite. Opera and music are also a huge part of their upbringing, and competitive skaters especially were allowed to use the designers of the Bolshoi and Kirov ballet companies to create their fabulous costumes, and to have famous ballet choreographers working with their trainers to create their routines. This approach scandalised the judging fraternities in many other countries, (and even today has its critics), and completely changed the face of ice dancing. Russians are not afraid to skate from the heart, showing a real passion which sometimes confuses the judges when they are evaluating a standardised discipline.

One of my favourite memories of Russia comes from 2011, when the World Figure Skating Championships had to be relocated, at very short notice, from Japan to Moscow. This would have been a daunting operation for many member countries, but the Russian organizers took it in their stride and put on an amazing event.

In normal circumstances, the Opening Ceremony takes place on the first night of the Championships, in the ice arena itself, and immediately after it the skaters take the ice to start to compete. On this occasion the ceremony occupied the whole evening with an unprecedented extravaganza. We were all invited to a theatre capable of seating thousands, the whole auditorium of which had been transformed into a huge circus-like tent. In the ceiling there were circus acts being performed, with constantly changing performers, while on the stage we were treated to performances by the Bolshoi Ballet Company's world-famous dancers. The Red Army Choir sang for us, as well as star opera singers, and one amazing performance after another filled the stage with music, colour, and excitement. The atmosphere was electric – an unbelievable evening, especially considering the speed with which it was produced – and I cannot remember such an event being bettered in my skating career.

In the skating arena itself, security around the VIP seating area appeared extremely tight and a little later we found out why. President Vladimir Putin had arrived, unannounced, and taken a seat in the middle of the area, which we only realised when the security officers who had been standing on the stairs facing the ice suddenly revolved and were apparently staring at us! There was no fanfare or introduction of the President, so for some time the audience were unaware he was there and then suddenly started to applaud when they noticed him. President Putin appeared to enjoy the performances and afterwards left the same way he had come, in three helicopters (two were decoys).

During that same Championships Bobby and I had our own 'special' evening. Tatiana Tarasova, the world-famous coach, had long been a friend of both of us. Our paths had crossed endlessly over the years, and she wanted to make our stay in Moscow even more memorable. (Her late husband - sadly he died during our visit - was an internationally renowned pianist and the world's best-known exponent of Rachmaninov. He was also our friend, and once when he was giving a recital in London, he came over to see us; during our rollicking evening together, he demolished a full bottle of whiskey then left for his hotel steady as a rock. Happy memories!).

Tatiana has become one of the most famous TV stars in Russia with her own skating show and her face on virtually every billboard in the city. As we arrived in Moscow she called to say, "I take you to the Bolshoi." True to her word, she did so - and in typical style, picking us up in her huge range Rover with three mink jackets on the back seat. She drove with scant regard for anything like speed limits to the theatre, where they just opened the gates for her, and we continued right up to the entrance. There she changed into another mink jacket, then treated us to strawberries and champagne before we took our seats while Tatiana waved to all her fans in the audience.

When the interval was announced we got a wonderful surprise. Unbeknown to us, Tatiana had invited many of the best Russian championship dance couples, whom of course we knew, and seated them among the audience. Their presence was then announced, and they all came over and joined us to the public's applause. Dear Tatiana is a STAR bar none all over the world, and a very kind lady - we are honoured to be considered amongst her friends.

Chapter 9: Further Adventures Abroad

Just send the ticket – I'll be there!

In the late Seventies, while Russian skaters were dominating the world scene and changing the face of ice dancing forever, Bobby was appointed as the official ice dance coach to the leading Japanese couple of that era, Noriko Sato and Tadayuki (Taiho) Takahashi. During his close collaboration with them and the Japanese Skating Federation, he coached them throughout their skating career from being the first Japanese couple to win an International Ice Dance competition until the ultimate achievement of representing their country in the 1984 Olympic Winter Games in Sarajevo, the year our mutual friends Jayne and Chris won their famous Gold Medal.

Over the intervening years both Taiho and Noriko married different partners and, at the same time, became famous all over Japan with their own ice extravaganza. Noriko has also made a name for herself as a choreographer for Japanese figure and pair skating, and for ice shows.

When they were training with Bobby in London, they rented the mews house next door to us and skated mainly at the recently opened Lee Valley Ice Centre, where they soon became a very popular part of the UK's then thriving skating scene. Like most Japanese, they were devoted to their sport, so they enjoyed watching all the skating events taking place around the country and making many new friends. Bobby has always hailed them as two of the nicest, most generous and hardworking couples he's ever had the pleasure of teaching and formed a close bond with their charming parents as well.

During and since that period, Bobby made at least sixteen trips to Japan; and I've made at least a dozen visits to this fascinating country for meetings, World Championships, and competitions. (We've also been lucky enough to visit South Korea and China as well, drink in their different cultures and meet many fascinating people). Needless to say, we're both great admirers of the Japanese culture and people and have enormously happy memories of our trips there. Everywhere - on the streets and in homes - is scrupulously clean. Schoolchildren are perfectly behaved, well dressed and so polite and organized. The public too are brought up to conform to the highest standards of courtesy and uniformity never seen in Western society. It must be a great place in which to live and work.

I remember on one trip Bobby, Lawrence Demmy and myself were invited to a private lunch given by a lady whom Bobby had been teaching at Queens, unaware that she was a very important businesswoman. We duly arrived and were ushered into a private room. To our surprise, our hostess, beautifully dressed in a silk kimono, was almost prostrate on the floor - the highest honour a lady can bestow on her guests. Normally, the Japanese bow to a certain level depending on their connection to their guests and their status, something instilled from birth. This lady wanted to show how pleased she was that we had accepted the invitation! What would you do if your hostess greeted you this way? We had no idea. Do you kneel down and help her to her feet? Stretch down and shake her hand and wait to see what she does? She was such a charming hostess we were completely mystified, and so afraid of being rude that we simply waited until she got up.

The next test was when we were served with a special Japanese meal. Protocol dictates that the most honoured guest sits at the head of the table, closest to a beautiful flower that dominates the table; so Bobby was seated there with the single bloom behind him, while Lawrence and I sat opposite each other, and our hostess seated at the other end.

The Japanese are so polite that if you don't eat something, they leave it in case you might like it later. Completely unsure of what was being put in front of me, I realised, as the meal progressed, that I was surrounded by about eight bowls of hardly touched Japanese delicacies. I was also suffering from cramp as the table was so low, and I was dying to stand up!

When we left, we agreed to meet for supper in the skating dining room then have an early night ready for the long day ahead.

Later, as we were woofing down a large supper in the official dining room, we were informed that a member of the Royal Family was giving a dinner that evening and we had to be ready, dressed in our special official blazers etc, to leave in thirty minutes. In Japan, and particularly when invited by royalty, you do not refuse. So off we went for the third meal of the busy day!

On a later trip, Noriko and Taiho's parents invited us to a special dinner in our honour in a very prestigious old restaurant. We'd never seen them before in their national dress and were amazed to see them both beautifully attired in kimonos, kneeling in front of their parents to greet us on arrival.

Our hosts had employed two Geisha girls to entertain us - magnificently made-up and attired girls who spend many years training to be, literally, additional hostesses. As we ate, served by a very elderly lady on her knees, they sat beside us feeding us food and drink and speaking in a special language they use at work, which sounds like birds singing.

Unfortunately for me, the national drink, *sake*, is served in square wooden cups. The more I was fed by the Geisha girls the more I dribbled so, after a while, it felt like it was disappearing into the breast pocket of my jacket. I think they had to haul me to my feet at the end of a magnificent meal, one we'll both remember until the end of our days – it was so beautifully presented and such a great honour, like stepping back two thousand years into the past.

On another visit there was another special dinner to entertain the guests, attended by Bobby, Lawrence and myself. This time it was at a local restaurant and, instead of sitting on the floor, the low tables had a trench underneath so you could almost sit properly with your legs down the hole. Things started off well - I hadn't drunk too much *sake*, knowing now how potent it was! But when the speeches began, I got a bad attack of cramp. So I said to Lawrence, seated opposite, "Lawrence, don't worry, but I'm just about to put my foot in your crotch. Try not to look too surprised." That, of course, set us both into a fit of giggles, (being a very important guest, Lawrence tried to mask them, without much success). The evening finished when I had to roll on the floor to extricate my feet from the hole and make an ignominious exit.

Many years prior to that, when Bobby was teaching at Queens Ice Club, he would retire during the break for a dance interval to rest in the café with a coffee and a smoke. During such breaks he got talking to a charming elderly Japanese gentleman, who said how much he enjoyed skating and ballroom dancing and their chats.

Some years later, Bobby was in Tokyo for a major international event. At an official practice session his (British) couple weren't doing very well, and tempers got frayed. Suddenly, a Japanese lady came up and asked him to follow her. Still uptight, Bobby explained that he was very busy but would accompany her when the session finished. The lady meekly sat down and waited.

When it was over, she said something he didn't quite understand. He went with her nonetheless, up to the top of the stadium, and into a room where he was amazed to see the Japanese gentleman with whom he used to have a daily coffee, seated surrounded by other gentlemen. It turned out that he was the brother of the Emperor of Japan!

The woman beside him immediately dropped to her knees in a deep bow. Bobby realised that he should bow too. He had actually asked a member of the Royal Family of Japan to wait until he'd finished - like asking the Duke of Edinburgh to hang on a few minutes until he was free!

Bobby was then asked to bring his British ice dance couple upstairs for the Emperor's brother to meet them again. Ken Foster and Kay Barsdell were duly collected. The whole solemnity of the occasion was spoilt when Kay greeted him with, "Hullo, how are you?" - the entourage nearly fainted at such familiarity. However, he was charming as ever and we all had a good laugh about it later.

My own personal connection with Japan spans some six decades. Whilst training at Richmond Ice Rink, I met one of the first Japanese ladies to compete in international events: a very young and charming Junko Hiramatsu. Little did we realise how our paths would cross again and again in later years!

After a highly successful competitive career, Junko started to judge and referee for her country and rose to become a very active and influential member of the ruling Japanese Skating Federation. She organized many events and remained a fixture in the skating scene during the years of her marriage and bringing up a family, latterly moving higher still and becoming a member, like myself, of the ISU Council.

I remember when I attended an earlier Championship in Tokyo, the ISU office holders were to be seated in a special area because the Crown Prince and Princess were attending that afternoon and would be joining us. They, (now the Emperor and Empress), were seated directly in front of us and proved to be very interested in the whole event, chatting in perfect English to the other members of their party and their hosts. The event was being held in a very large stadium seating about ten thousand people. When the Royal Party was announced, the whole audience rose as one and bowed - producing a sea of black, as there were very few grey-haired people in the audience. An awesome spectacle.

When the last World Championships were held in Tokyo in 2019, Junko was there to welcome us. Holding a prime position on the organizing committee, she arranged wonderful official dinners and other cultural events during the Championships, fortuitously held at the most beautiful time of the year, Cherry Blossom Time - an unimaginable spectacle which couldn't be replicated anywhere else in the world. It was also a memorable event for the minor earthquake during one of the official lunches, when the whole table moved sideways then returned to its original position. Hardly anyone commented on it as it happens so often, (which I found almost as disconcerting as my place setting suddenly moving sideways and back again!).

I think, dear readers, Japan and its skaters will always occupy a very special place in our hearts.

We also both have vivid memories of the trips we made to

Israel. Annually, for a number of years, an international skating competition was held in the country's northernmost town, Metula, close to the Lebanese border and the Golan Heights, where we could clearly see the rockets passing overhead.

There was a friendly atmosphere between the residents and those across the border, with a special gate opened daily to allow Lebanese workers to come in and work, despite the continual state of war between Israel and Palestine almost next door. Nearly every home had an underground shelter, and every night the sky was alight with rockets flying between the two – an amazing but rather daunting situation for visitors!

However, the Skate Israel Competition was organized by benefactors Yossi and Galia Goldberg, who were the most wonderful hosts, and it was always a pleasure to be invited. The Ice Rink complex also included a swimming pool, practice rooms, a fully equipped gym and a restaurant. One unusual feature was that the end wall of the rink was made completely of glass. Yossi explained that the view we saw through it was the hill upon which Joshua had preached to the multitude, and the Sea of Galilee where Jesus preached to His disciples.

A great fan of speed skating, a branch which received considerable support from him, as a member of the Knesset, (the Israeli Parliament), Yossi and his guests were afforded entry to holy sites that weren't generally open to the public. On one occasion he took us to Nazareth, where we saw what is acknowledged to be the home of Jesus. He also took us to a simple basement with stone seating around its unadorned, whitewashed walls, into which the public weren't normally allowed, and told us that it was one of the oldest synagogues where Christ Himself had preached! It was an amazing and very memorable feeling to be in a sacred place of such age and gave us a sense of peace we will never forget.

Yossi also took us to one of the oldest Kibbutz in the country. It was fascinating to see how it worked, with everyone basically equal; even high-ranking Army officers took their turn to work on the farm, cook and wash up, and serve food in the large restaurant, and all the cars on site could be used by anyone – if they needed a car, they just picked the nearest one and off they went! Old people were treated with great respect and cared for throughout their lives. Mobile electric wheelchairs were parked near restaurants and other facilities for senior citizens to use at will; and they, in return, looked after the young children while their parents were working. What a great idea for the modern world. There was no need for money, everyone was well cared-for, and peace and happiness pervaded the place – it was a lesson to all of us lucky enough to make such a visit.

Sadly, Yossi passed away some years ago, but his legacy lives on.

Chapter 10: The 'Boston Boat Party'

Life can steal our fortunes but never our memories.

The ISU Congress, at which elections to office were decided, was normally held every four years, but the most recent congresses had decided that these elective congresses would in future be held to coincide with the years of the Winter Olympic Games – thus after the 1992 Davos Congress in Switzerland, elections would be held again in Boston, Massachusetts, two years later, and thereafter every fourth year.

In 1994, the Congress would be momentous because the incumbent President, Olaf Poulsen, would be stepping down after a very long and distinguished service, and his successor to the office would be appointed. In those far-off days the choice of President was discussed by the Council and once chosen, the new President was elected simply by acclamation, without opposition. This took place before the long sessions of voting for positions on the many committees and advisory committees began, and the election of the President had always followed this procedure.

Lawrence Demmy, retired from competition with his partner Jean Westwood after winning four World and European Ice Dance Championships, was the expected candidate to take over. He'd had a lifetime's experience in the sport, having risen to become chairman of the Ice Dance Committee and then to his current position as ISU Vice-President; and having received intimation that the Council would propose him when the time came, had planned his life accordingly. A very successful businessman based in Hull, East Yorkshire, he decided to retire in order to concentrate on promoting the ISU all over the world and bringing in many new ideas he felt were important to the growth of all its disciplines. With that aim in mind, he and his wife Pamela decided it would be advantageous to live in London, close to Heathrow Airport, because of the extra travelling that his new position would entail.

As Vice-President, Lawrence had been asked to make the speech at the closing banquet thanking the outgoing President Poulsen for his dedication to the sport, and to present him with a gold Rolex watch as a measure of the Council's gratitude. He had also personally proposed the introduction of a new rule that the ex-President and his wife would be guests of the ISU at any Championship or event they chose to attend in future, and this had been accepted.

As a member of the Ice Dance Committee, my name had gone forward, with others, to be considered for election to the new committee. (I'd been elected to the Ice Dance Committee in Davos, along with my friend and colleague Ann Shaw, and was thoroughly enjoying being able to have a positive influence over the discipline closest to my heart and experience). That's when it all went pear-shaped! The ISU has always been a very political organization, and certain factions were about to rear their heads. A member of the Council representing Italy, Ottavio Cinquanta, had been suggested as a candidate President by a group of office holders who had decided that he should stand against Lawrence, and had been working behind the scenes, in great secrecy, to achieve their aim.

On the night before the elections, our hosts, the United States Figure Skating Association, invited all the guests to join them on a boating trip in the bay. We all duly boarded the ship, and I couldn't understand why so few were taking advantage of the magnificent views of Boston from the decks. Everyone seemed huddled in little groups on the various decks and not eating much, and it wasn't until the next day that we realised why - plots were afoot well into the early hours of the morning...

The business and elections to all appointments takes the whole final day, right up until the official banquet which closes the Congress before we all leave for home. Bobby had been sitting in Lawrence and Pam's suite with Pam, not knowing how things were going and getting gently inebriated in the process, but ready to celebrate Lawrence's elevation, at last, to the Presidency and, hopefully, my re-election to the Ice Dance Committee.

Neither happened! To the surprise of many, including the

main body of Congress, the election of the new President would not be by acclamation as in the past. Instead, a late proposal was passed to decide the office by a full congressional vote – which Lawrence lost by six votes, 46:52, to Ottavio Cinquanta. It was a tremendous disappointment; the next World Championships were due to be held in Birmingham, West Midlands, and we had all so hoped that, as the new President, it would be Lawrence acting as host to skaters and officials from all over the skating world.

When it came to the election for the Ice Dance Committee, I lost my seat to someone who would become a life-long friend, the late Ludmila Michailovskaya. (I regained it two years later and held it until my elevation to the Council in 2002 in Kyoto, Japan - the first person, I believe, ever to be re-elected after being voted off a committee!). Not the outcome any of us had hoped for, and it was like a wake when we returned to the suite. But we pulled ourselves together and, like the troopers we were, entered the Ballroom with heads held high, (if tails between legs).

Looking back, it seems amazing that one boat trip around Boston Bay could change the fortunes of the ISU for decades to come. Lawrence Demmy had mentored us both, Bobby from the age of fourteen and me in my later teen years when I began to compete. His knowledge of the sport was immense, he'd overseen enormous changes in all its disciplines, and was greatly respected worldwide. He made an outstanding speech and presented the gold watch to Olaf Poulsen and wished the new President every success in the chair. Ironically, in the months and years after that miserable evening, Lawrence admitted that the choice of Ottavio Cinquanta had probably been the right one! Had he been elected, the enormous amount of travelling might have adversely affected his marriage, which was far more important to him than holding office. He often said that Ottavio had made a very business-like President who completely revolutionised the ISU into the forward-thinking organization it is today. As Vice-President, Lawrence gave Ottavio total support throughout the rest of his career until his retirement; in fact, they became firm friends, often discussing changes and proposals they felt would be advantageous to the Union.

Sadly, Lawrence passed away after a long illness in 2016. He made a great difference to both of us and the skating world in general, and his contribution will always remain part of the Union's history. He will never be forgotten.

When the opening notes of the ISU Fanfare were heard at the NEC Stadium in Birmingham for the 1995 World Championships, it was the culmination of a dream for me that had started in Streatham Ice Rink in the mid-Seventies with the first International Competition, (sponsored by Prestige Cutlery), which had attracted skaters in all four disciplines from all over the world.

In the intervening two decades the NSA had come to the forefront of international skating with a competition at Richmond Ice Rink sponsored by companies like St Ivel International and Skate Electric International. By the early Nineties this NSA annual event was the premier competition to start the season in October, and nearly every future European and World Champion had participated in it. These large events gave us a very good grounding in organization and management, as well as all the pitfalls as events began including more and more referees, judges and skaters from all over the world, although by present day standards, our methods were archaic! We had a solid group of volunteers and virtually no paid staff, to maximise the profit margin for each event. There would be a basic organizing committee with sub-committees for transport, hotels, social events, closing banquet or dinner and so forth, the heads of which invited others to join them. Wonderful non-skaters and skaters, some no longer with us, were the mainstays: Eileen Anderson, Joan Wallis, Nada Mrdalj, Chloe Ronaldson, Vanessa Riley, Kay Robinson, Helen Poole, and so many, many others too numerous to mention here - and that's how it all came together. The central office kept all the records, we had a team of amateur specialists in the marking system, everyone worked as a team, and we all had great fun – committee members even used their holiday time in order to help in this hey-day of our sport. (One of my roles was to flatter, cajole and threaten sponsors into supporting us, but it was always with the aim of bringing skating to the fore both in the UK

and the rest of the world. I freely acknowledge that I 'used'
everyone!).

The last time the World Championships had been held in the
UK was in 1950, and my dream was to hold one again in England
before I finally retired. However, before that could even be
considered there were numerous hoops to jump through. The ISU
insisted that before a member could be considered as a host for a
World Championship, they had to hold a European Championship
first. Normally this could take years to achieve, as so many countries
wished to do so, but we had an ace card: Lawrence Demmy, who
was involved in the final choices for all the ISU events both in Speed
Skating and Figure Skating as well, of course, with the politics of the
Winter Olympic Games.

We accordingly applied to the ISU Council to host the 1989
European Championships, and after a few setbacks were successful.
When any member of the ISU family considers organising a major
event, only one name immediately springs to mind: Peter Krick. A
former competitive skater, Peter became an important advisor to the
Deutscher Eissport-Verband eV, with the bonus for us all of his
charming wife Sissy, who often accompanied him to events in her
capacity as an International Judge and Referee. Bobby and I are lucky
enough to have known Peter and Sissy for many years; long enough
to follow the progress of their children, (both of whom inherited
their parents' charm and personality, needless to say), from infancy to
adulthood, when their son became a High Court Judge and their
daughter an internationally famous medical specialist. We had the
pleasure of seeing in the new century with them when they came to
London for New Year 2000, and celebrated our long friendship
watching the marvellous firework display that heralded the beginning
of a new era.

For as long as I can remember Peter has been there, usually
somewhere behind the scenes, very efficiently and quietly making sure
everything runs like clockwork. His knowledge and experience in
running skating events – even the Winter Olympics, wherever they're
held - is encyclopaedic, as is that of the small team who invariably
accompany him. Our first port of call to plan the running of the

Championships, Peter went on to be appointed Chair of the ISU Sports Directorate from 2006 - 2014, an acknowledgement of the esteem in which he was held then and has been ever since, as he continues to be involved with events all over the world.

One night, Peter really saved the championships as far as we were concerned. All had been proceeding well. We had an ice surface in the main arena for the main event, and another in the adjoining stadium to act as the practice rink. Then, late one evening, I was hauled out of bed. A leak had been found in the practice rink and the ice was slowly ebbing away! Panic! I immediately called Peter. The first practice group was due to take the ice on that rink in about seven hours, so Peter and the group of engineers in charge sprang into action. He isolated the problem, then once it was mended, stayed up all night with a hose, carefully spraying the surface to rebuild the inches of ice required, hour after hour. With barely minutes to spare, the first practice group was able to start exactly on schedule, and what would've been a disaster for the immensely complex timetable was averted. Once again, Peter had saved the event as he's so often done over many years, and on behalf of everyone in the Union, I take this opportunity to thank him.

Meanwhile, the ISU appointed a 'Technical Delegate' to oversee the Championships and supervise our preparations, the late Josef Dedic, and as he had often worked in partnership with Peter, it made our preparations much easier. By then we were accustomed to organising large, sponsored skating events, but a Championship is quite different, and costs about £3 million (/€3.5 million/$4.1 million) to stage, A very long, detailed manual is produced by the ISU containing all the guidelines, every one of which must be strictly adhered to before the event can proceed. We then had about three years in which to find the finance, hotels, venues, form all the committees, and generally set it up based on the strict guidelines laid down by the ISU, which appointed one of their members as ISU Representative for the event to supervise all our preparations.

Finding a venue with hotel accommodation within easy reach and good transport connections to and from the airports was proving difficult. This event was a large step up from an International competition. We needed major sponsorship for the various areas but could not, under any circumstances in those days, have the actual ISU event sponsored. It was a whole new ball game and included hundreds of volunteers. To ensure that, in the event of a loss, it would not be against the NSA, we were advised to form a completely different limited company to take control. Ice Skating Promotions was duly formed and exists to this day; I believe it's still used as a charity arm in which funds can be gathered to help skaters with their expenses.

We were very honoured that the Princess Royal agreed to attend the 1989 Championships and to meet the skaters afterwards. It was the time of the Irish problems and security was unbelievably tight. Early in the morning the whole stadium was swept by teams and dogs. Then we were informed of the Princess's progress, minute by minute, as she travelled towards us so that we would be ready to greet Her Royal Highness on arrival at the front door and usher her upstairs as quickly as possible. The large reception room had floor to ceiling windows, and I was told that on no account was I to allow the Princess, (who had arrived unexpectedly accompanied by her young daughter Zara), to go anywhere near them.

All the guests were assembled in the main room where tea was to be served, and rather embarrassed, I stood with Princess Anne and Zara in the middle of the room. The rest of the guests, uncertain what to do, were ringed around us so it was a little like feeding time at the zoo, with me trying to signal for the guests to join us. Finally, some got the message and moved towards us, to my infinite relief! Both were charming guests, and the Princess took Zara with her onto the ice to meet the skaters on the strict understanding that, "she held Mr. Jones's hand and then she could come with us." I still have a photograph of the occasion, and now Zara is a mother herself, it brings back happy memories whenever I see her and her family in the press.

(Sometime later, I was invited to a banquet at the Mansion House at which Princess Anne was the Guest of Honour. It was a very smart affair, but being a nobody, I was seated by the kitchen door with the Princess's protection officer, and we had a very interesting meal discussing the Birmingham visit, where he'd been on duty that day, and how difficult his job could be, especially for a woman, due to the long hours - added to the fact that all the officers had to ski well, because many members of the Royal Family are excellent skiers and at their most vulnerable whilst on the slopes).

Funding an operation like the European Championships takes money running into the millions, but with assistance from the ISU and various other sources we managed it. 'Black Friday' occurred just as the event was being staged, which meant that we made a small loss, but it didn't deter us from applying for the World Championship in hopes of recovering some finances. So when we were awarded the 1995 event, we mobilised the same teams of skating friends, plus many hundreds more; but this was a much, much larger operation with a budget of £3.5 million, and we had to search further for help.

Some sponsorship was permitted, and we were very lucky indeed to have Paul Zetter, CBE, and his wife Helen come on board. Paul was already the Chairman of the Sports Aid Foundation and wonderfully enthusiastic about the event and everything to do with young people and sport. Chairman of Zetters' Pools and based in the city near the offices of the skating association, Paul permitted our finance meetings to take place in his offices and kindly allowed us the use of his finance department to guide us through the pitfalls ready to trap a bunch of amateurs trying to organize a huge international event. It was a wonderful gesture and made our job so much easier.

We visited a number of suitable London venues which would have been the first option for such a prestigious event, including one now known as the O2 Arena, (it was then under construction), and even discussed housing everyone on a cruise ship anchored in the docks, and ferrying them back and forth by helicopter to avoid the London traffic! But in the end, we decided to return to the NEC in Birmingham, which had proved an excellent venue for the European Championships in 1989 and couldn't be bettered for road, rail and airport connections.

We accordingly took over the whole hotel that was within a short walk of the Centre and hired three stadia: the main Ice Pad, the Practice Rink, and a third hall for all the offices and press facilities, plus dressing rooms and an endless array of catering facilities and show stands selling merchandise. Nothing, not so much as a teaspoon, came with it - thus the forward planning was immense, because besides the actual ice pads and Zamboni Ice cleaners, everything else had to be ordered in or built up from scratch. Luckily, we'd learned a lot from organizing the European Championships in 1989, and Helen Day and her company joined us to help to plan the whole operation. Her knowledge of hosting these very large events proved invaluable, and she dealt with all the promotional aspects, ticket sales and other areas where we had little experience. (Helen and her staff had worked for many years with us planning the annual International Competition that opened the ISU programme for each season).

Nearly the whole Championship would be televised by the BBC and so they were brought into our planning meetings at a very early stage. For the first time in history, the first official event of the World Championships would be a concert of music connected with skating in all its forms. This came about because, as a youngster, I'd been a huge fan of a radio programme called *Friday Night is Music Night*. The programme itself had been running for decades and was almost an institution in the world of radio. I boldly approached the director and asked him if on the Friday night of the opening of the event, it could be staged in the Birmingham Concert Hall and feature the Birmingham City Orchestra, with famous skaters of the past actually singing in the whole presentation.

He was intrigued enough by the idea to make it happen! Robin Cousins, fresh from stage success in London's West End, agreed to perform, as did my old friend Anita Harris, who had been a competitive skater in her younger years. That evening, everyone attending the Championships progressed to the Concert Hall by buses which dropped them as close to the venue as possible. We then walked to the entrance through a path lined with fire-eaters, steel bands, jugglers, and children dressed in bright costumes, which made the entry rather different! The concert programme featured all sorts of music associated with skating and skaters: the Skaters' Waltz, of course, Don Quixote, world famous as John Curry's choice to win

Olympic Gold, and even some of the music I and my partners had skated to; but the climax was the whole orchestra playing Ravel's Bolero. Many of the those present had heard it played all over the world but had never *seen it performed* by a huge orchestra. Visually it was incredibly exciting, with a single musician, spot-lit in a dark theatre, playing the haunting opening melody. Then, as the minutes passed, the rest of the orchestra joined in until the climax created by the huge kettle-drums - then absolute silence.

The whole audience of skaters, judges, officials and spectators were on their feet and the reception was one I will never forget. I was so very proud that, after all these years, my dream of a 'Friday Night is Skating Night' had become a reality!

The next evening was the official opening of the World Championships. Immediately prior to the ceremony, the NSA was presented with a presidential regalia by the company who had crafted medals and trophies for all the major skating events for many decades: a beautiful medallion of gold, silver, and enamel, with the Association's insignia in the centre, and hung on a wide blue ribbon. As the event was the most important in the NSA's history for a very long time, I thought it appropriate to wear it for the opening, which was preceded by a cocktail party in my suite. Suitably arrayed, I began to greet guests at the door; but my natural vanity was soon eclipsed when a very dear friend entered, exclaiming, "Darling! I just love your necklace – but have you got the matching ear-rings?" Completely deflated, I took it off, returned it to the showcase, and abandoned the whole idea – a lesson about vanity I never forgot.

Once again, music was the main theme of the opening ceremony on the big night, with hundreds of skaters in Victorian costume welcoming Queen Victoria onto the ice in a beautifully decorated sleigh, surrounded by happy young skaters. Around the rink itself we welcomed the band of the Coldstream Guards, who marched around the perimeter of the ice surface wearing their bearskins and playing marches, including my request, '*Blaze Away,*' while synchronised skaters performed in authentic Beefeater costumes, (well drilled by Jenni Smith and her husband Mike Smith, who were then very instrumental in bringing this discipline to Britain)

- the first time both the ice and the surrounding areas were made part of the ceremony, giving a highly successful overall effect.

The whole event was televised and watched by large audiences both at home and in the stadia, where Canada's Elvis Stojko won the Men's competition, Lu Chen of China the Ladies', and Radka Kovarikova and Rene Novotny of Czechoslovakia the Pairs, with the Ice Dance title taken by the Russian couple Oksana Grischuk and Evgeni Platov.

The Championships concluded with a gala dinner, with Joe Loss and his Orchestra playing until well after midnight in the hotel ballroom. We were all sad to see the event come to an end after so many new friendships had been forged, (more than two hundred and fifty helpers from all over the country had contributed to this resounding success), and it had been enjoyed by everyone. The President of the ISU said for some years afterwards that it had been the best championships ever held, (a comment which riled several fellow ISU members when it was voiced in their company, but made me personally very pleased indeed!); and it made a very handsome profit to benefit skaters for many years to come, which made all the preparations well worthwhile.

Naturally, I was delighted that my dream had come true in such a wonderful way – and on that happy note, it was time to leave the stage.

Chapter 11: Night of the Long Knives

Success is the best revenge

After the UK's success in hosting two Championships, one European and one World, and prompted by the Olympic Gold Medal wins of Jeannette Altwegg, John Curry, Robin Cousins and Jane Torvill and Christopher Dean, the sports arm of the Government decided to inject some funds into skating at long last. Until that point, there had been no money from the NSA to back British talent. Chris and Jayne had been working full-time as a policeman and insurance clerk respectively when they won their first British Ice Dance title in 1978, until a very unusual and generous award of £60,000 from Nottingham City Council, (£300,000/€349,200/$414,400 today), enabled them to give up work and concentrate on skating; John and Robin both had to find wealthy sponsors; all four had to leave the UK - Torvill and Dean to Oberstdorf, Germany, and Curry and Cousins to the USA – to get the quality of training and coaching they required – a sad situation, and long overdue for a change.

Now, in return for funding, the Sports Council, (rebranded in 1998 to UK Sport and Sport England), expected a say in the management of what was, to be honest, a rather old-fashioned, top-heavy organization heavily reliant on volunteers to promote the sport and fund the skaters, as should have been done by the Association. We had achieved a great deal, including the highly respected annual International Competition in October, which opened the major championship season, and since every ensuing World Champion in all four disciplines competed, gave an indication of the form skaters needed to achieve. Nonetheless, I agreed that it was time for a complete overhaul. Now, the Sports Council would require representation on the board and someone they considered suitable as General Secretary, since they'd be contributing towards the salary. A trouble-shooter was duly appointed to bring the NSA into the twentieth century, shake up all existing practices and in-house committees and oversee and implement changes as soon as possible.

It happened in quite a ruthless manner. The first course of action was to separate the ice skaters and roller skaters, who had previously operated as one body with a board of directors elected from both sides. Now, the President would remain in place and become Chairman of the main board, with two new separate boards, the Federation for Ice Skating, both figure and speed, (FIS), and the Federation for Roller Skating, (FRS), with entirely separate accounts.

In theory it was a sensible plan, but in practice it didn't really work. It effectively ended the close co-operation between ice and roller skaters, both in public and in private, which had existed since our sports' earliest years. We had always enjoyed helping each other with fundraising ventures and profiting equally from the successes - indeed, the relationship between the disciplines was so close that ice skating judges often judged roller skating too. Not any longer. While the ice board would remain centrally situated as before, the roller board had to find new headquarters – with no cost involved! – and were denied any say in the composition of the NSA staff, (now renamed NISA GB, the National Ice Skating Association of Great Britain).

Then after a reasonably tactful period had elapsed, the roller skaters were consigned to oblivion, told to run their own show and not to expect any real funding. The reason? They were not an Olympic sport, nor likely to be in the foreseeable future, and therefore expendable. How sad for the discipline, and for the UK's young roller skaters! But despite this dismissive attitude, roller skating continues to thrive all over the world under the leadership of Mrs Margaret Brooks. Thanks largely due to determined fundraising by skaters' parents, Artistic Roller Skating and Roller Speed Skating attract huge numbers of participants, especially in Spain, Italy and South America; thousands of competitors, (rather than the hundreds typical for ice), take part in its international championships, while British coaches are regarded as among the best in the world. An extremely difficult sport in which to achieve success, it's a shame that it has never been featured on TV in any depth.

What the Sports Council failed to realise is that the ISU is a highly political organization, with new members from other countries constantly joining and making the Union ever richer and more important. Therefore, if you want to be awarded prestigious, money-making international events, it behoves you to maintain a 'presence' at said events and do some entertaining in return. Business is always done at a high level between Presidents and General Secretaries, so it was essential for Great Britain to be represented as Lawrence Demmy did with great success for many years until his retirement from the Association and appointment as ISU Honorary Vice President. (At that time, the General Secretary of the NSA was not usually present at international events but assisted when events were held in the UK).

In 1995, when the balance of power changed, it should have been realised that this representation was a vital part of the 'job description.' For the next few years, new Presidents and General Secretaries, (the title changed in 2010 to Chief Executives), seemed to recognise this, and did their best to attend as many events as possible, resulting in the Association being awarded the European Figure Skating Championships in 2012. However, following this very successful event, British officers became less and less visible at major events held in Europe, North America and the Far East, to the point where these days their attendance is rare to non-existent. As far as I'm concerned, these two posts should be occupied only by people willing to fulfil their demands, bear the exposure, and constantly work to promote skaters and skating internationally as well as at home - like Ken Pendrey, chairman of the speed skating arm and NISA, who continued to oversee and promote speed skating within Great Britain and abroad, gaining many successes for the discipline and becoming the doyen of speed skating on ice.

During the run-up to the 1995 championships, I'd made it very plain that immediately afterwards, at the next AGM, I would step down as President and Chairman to indulge my hobby of trying to introduce Synchronised Skating into the UK, (I had just offered myself to be part of that new committee, but inferred that I'd happily remain on the Ice Dance Committee as well if it was felt that I could continue to help). This would give others the opportunity to take over and carry on the work of promoting ice and roller skating at all levels worldwide.

Said AGM was held at London's famous Savoy Hotel, (where else?), and lasted six hours. Voting for all positions had been held previously and I strongly supported the nomination for President of Sally Anne Stapleford, a past champion and current ISU office holder whom I thought ideally suited to the job.

By then, I'd served as Ice Dance Committee Chairman, Chairman of Council, Chairman of the Board, and then President, for almost nineteen years, plus two years on the ISU Ice Dance Committee, and had every intention of trying to regain the seat I'd lost in Boston at the 1996 elections – although I'd been told by my friends, (and enemies!), that despite my belief that everyone loved me, and such a thing could never happen, I'd been on the scene for too long and the natives were getting restless.

After I made my farewell speech, the AGM proceeded. I was very pleased that Sally was elected to take over; but then sure enough, as my friends had predicted, it became obvious that I was *persona non grata*. Not elected to any position except a seat on the Synchronised Committee, (which everyone thought would amount to nothing – wrong again!), it was four hours before one of the elder and more gracious members remembered to rise and thank me for my nineteen years of service - which I missed, having gone for an overdue pee.

Within days, I received a letter from the General Secretary telling me that I was to be relieved of my seat on the British Olympic Association, even though I only had two months left to run before leaving anyway, and that I would not be included in the British delegation for the ISU Congress later that year, 'since I no longer held any office in the association and, in particular, in Ice Dancing.' That meant I couldn't be nominated for the vacant seat on the Ice Dance Committee when it came up for grabs in Davos – the 'New Order' really had done a hatchet job, just as my friends had warned, and it looked like curtains for me as far as the ISU was concerned.

I don't take rejection very well, so I hatched a plot. They'd forgotten that I was still a member of the Synchronised Committee – which happily nominated me to be their representative on the delegation. It went down like a lead balloon, but there was nothing they could do about it and they were stuck with me!

To get their own back, they sat me at the end of our table at Congress, (each delegation has a table with their country's name on it), and no-one spoke to me there, or at mealtimes at the hotel, nor was I invited to the daily delegates' meetings to discuss the day's agenda. Those who shunned me were a little taken aback to see how many delegates from other countries came up to chat with me instead of with the new members they didn't really know; and furious when Dr Montag, President of the German Federation, very kindly nominated me for the Ice Dance Committee place, as another member country was allowed to do in those days (it's changed since).

When I won the seat back, the only delegation - amounting to more than six hundred people – who didn't rise to applaud my success was, you guessed it, the British. Adding insult to injury for them, and surprise and honour for me, the ISU President descended from his seat on the dais and traversed the length of the hall to congratulate me personally. Their faces could have curdled milk.

Sadly, my fellow delegates continued not to speak to me, and I dined alone until we all left – but once re-elected, I served on the committee until 2002 when I was elected to the ISU Council - where I continued to serve till I retired, due to age, in 2010. Success is the best revenge!

Postscript: some years later, when we were living in Spain, Helen Poole (Volgushev) came to stay, bearing a message from the latest General Secretary, of whom there had been a succession in the intervening years, installed at Head Office. It said that the Association 'no longer wished to live in the past,' (despite my past including five Gold British Ice Dance Championship Medals, five Gold Medals and one Silver for the European Ice Dance Championships, and four Gold and one Silver World Championship Medals – a total of fourteen Gold and two Silver, all achieved with two different partners). 'To achieve this aim,' the message went on, 'the portraits of all the past Presidents that have adorned the walls of the headquarters over many years are to be returned to the President concerned,' (a difficult operation as the first one was installed in the nineteenth century!), 'or destroyed.'.

I sent a very polite reply suggesting that my offending portrait be disposed of in a clinically impossible place; and since I was really uninterested in what became of it, Helen subsequently collected it and disposed of it on my behalf.

Chapter 12: Creating a Winning Performance

Lose the flash and lose the trash

I'm including this chapter mainly for the benefit of aspiring champion skaters and their coaches, to pass on some of the tips I've gleaned over my decades of association with competitive skating - though I hope it will interest general readers too.

To begin on a musical note: the incomparable John Curry once said, "All skaters, either with a partner, solo, or in a team, are Ice Dancers." I certainly appreciate this sentiment, because whatever your choice of discipline, when competing in our special sport, you are indeed a dancer! Skating is one of the very few Olympic sports which requires the competitor to use music of their own choice - a choice considered by the judges when assessing that performance, and therefore of paramount importance.

Music was first heard on ice as part of a performance when the nineteenth century American ballet dancer and figure skater Jackson Haines decided to add it to his routines. Haines, also a keen ballroom dancer, used his skills to transform the sport; and as ballroom dancing became all the rage during the Twenties and Thirties, couples on ice followed suit. As the twentieth century progressed, music became ever more closely associated with skating, which in turn was popularised by the films of the legendary Norwegian figure skater Sonja Henie, winner of more Olympic and World titles than any other lady in ice skating history. (By 1940, Henie was also one of Hollywood's highest-paid stars, with numerous box-office hits to her credit including *Thin Ice*, *My Lucky Star* and *Sun Valley Serenade*).

By this time, music had become an essential part of a skating performance; indeed, nowadays they are inseparable, with some skaters venturing into music specially composed for them and, in some cases, played by one of the partners. Compared with the years in which I was competing, not only is the standard of skating light years better now, but the choice of music is also much more varied.

Skaters in all disciplines must be in tip-top physical condition - basically, superb athletes – and their music must enhance their best points and showcase their creative ability while staying within the rules laid down by the governing body. However, they must still *entertain* their judges as well as their audience, and this is something both coaches and skaters sometimes forget. Often, after a big event, dancers would come to me, maybe as the referee, and ask why they didn't get the higher marks they thought they deserved. I usually told them it was because their music hadn't been popular either with the audience or the judges, and therefore had not been a good choice musically for their routine. If I asked why they'd chosen it, the invariable reply was that they'd 'felt' the music and wanted to show that side of their personality. My usual response was they'd forgotten that they were athletes who also had to entertain the public - and that's what makes memorable, medal-winning routines so hard to create. In a stadium seating ten thousand people or more, those at the back can't see faces or the finer points of interpretation, but still need to understand what the skaters are trying to do and enjoy the bigger picture from their more distant vantage point. Skating is more than theatre on four sides, it's close-up and far away at the same time; that's why costume, makeup and facial expressions are all essential parts of the act, and all require emphasising to get over to the public - win their vote and you're more than halfway there.

It's different in other sports. For instance, a sprinter doesn't need make-up, a special costume or acting ability to become the fastest in the world, whereas in skating, we *do* need all these extra things – it's showtime! I speak as one who knows. In our early days of no TV, no agents, and poor lighting, it was vital to make a big impact the moment you stepped onto the ice. Both my leading ladies knew that and, poor girls, had to match my ego, (as big as the Grand Canyon). We became past masters at making sure we weren't ignored, on or off the ice. If you want to be a star, *be* one - on *and* off the ice!

I believe that when you choose your music, it must be something you *want* to perform as well as being innovative yet understandable to the public and judges – enjoyable and entertaining in itself before you even set foot on ice to interpret it. Your performance is the icing on the cake, so choose your cake with great care because it's the engine which will drive your wonderful presentation. Looking back over the many great performances I've witnessed in my lifetime I often remember them decades later by the name of the music as well as the skating. That's why it's so important! Music has the power to transfix an audience with its dexterity, colour and beauty. Skaters have the power to transfix an audience with their own amazing physical ability, beauty, and interpretation. Put the two together and you have a formidable combination – but remember that simply keeping in time with your chosen melody does *not* mean you're interpreting the piece, merely showing your technical skills. To interpret successfully, you need to exercise more subtle talents and match each other in demonstrating your *feeling* for the melody.

The judges are unlikely to be trained musicians, (useful though that would be), but will have had very careful instructions during the official seminars, plus a lifetime of experience, enabling them to adjudicate on the choice of the music in line with the regulations. However, an ice dancing judge may be very hard pushed, on top of all the other parts of the skaters' performance, to be sure that the musical choice is well thought out.

In my distant day, when we competed in ice dance events at home or abroad the music to which we all skated was essentially the same. Our only available option was to select a rhythm and tune and have it played and recorded by Dougie Walker, the superb organist who played at the Nottingham Ice Stadium. (Nearly every rink in the country then had a resident organist, band or pianist, and the organ is a wonderful instrument for an ice rink with its wide range of effects and outstanding sound). Everyone's Free Dance followed the same accepted pattern: a fast piece followed by a slow piece and ending with a fast piece, and I remember sitting on the stool at the organ with Dougie, discussing our music for the forthcoming competition season. As I read music, I could discuss what were, for him, quite unusual deviations like ceasing the melody while continuing the beat, or starting the performance with only drum beats for the first thirty seconds, (we tried that, got shot down in flames by the judges, and had to abandon the idea before even starting the international events), or not having the pieces recorded in the same order, or introducing different sound effects.

He flatly refused to budge from his normal Fast, Slow, Fast. So June and I went out and bought a record of music played by Joe Loss and his dance orchestra, and took it to an engineer who recorded it the way we wanted – thereby taking the ice dance world by storm because no couple had ever dared to do this before, and it was a huge change as far as the judges were concerned. However, it worked brilliantly, albeit with the sad unforeseen consequence that the next year, nearly everyone else followed suit and Dougie, for whom I had and always will have the greatest respect, was out of a job recording music for Free Dances.

Music for Free Dancing then took on a completely new aspect, revolutionised again years later by Torvill and Dean's 'Bolero,' the first time a whole Free Dance routine was performed to a single piece - an enduring reminder of the power of music which has since morphed into the exciting range of possibilities open to ice dancers of today.

If you aspire to be a champion skater, you could learn a lot about pushing the boundaries from that supreme showman, violinist and conductor Andre Rieu and his Johann Strauss Orchestra. I bow to none in my total admiration for Rieu, who plays to hundreds of thousands all over the world and presents his orchestra in a way unsurpassed by any other entrepreneur, which has young and old alike getting up and dancing in the aisles. Music can have that effect if selected properly, even without the added attraction of skating - not that I'm suggesting the audiences at ice dance events should get up and dance too, nice idea though it is!

Unless you've seen Rieu in action, you can't imagine the visual effects he creates to complement the music he plays. He once flew a complete life-size reproduction of Vienna's Schönbrunn Palace to an Australian venue - the world's biggest-ever stage set – and when it was re-assembled, a hundred ballroom dancers in evening dress danced in full view of the upstairs windows while the orchestra played on the terrace below; on one side was a rink with dozens of skaters on the ice and on the other side were fountains moving in time with the music. Other such spectacular performances with fantastic music and costumes have taken place in North and South America, and many other parts of the world, and I feel that all skaters should view them - not to use the same type of music when they skate, but as a lesson in how to perform to any rhythm.

Remember, there's no better combination than ice and music (unless it's ice and gin and tonic!).

Turning to Compulsory Dances: I've been involved with these difficult exercises throughout my skating career both on and off the ice, first as a skater, then as a Championship competitor, and later as a judge and referee. (I also created two new ones, the Silver Samba and Starlight Waltz, with my colleague Peri Horne). During my tenure on the ISU Ice Dance Committee, I helped to refine and improve the rules and regulations of Compulsory Dances and their execution, as well as their evolution; and finally, as a member of the ISU Council, I was entrusted by the President to find a solution when the International Olympic Committee instructed that the number of Ice Dance events in the Winter Olympic Games had to be reduced from three to two. The President wished the change to include some of the existing elements of the Compulsory Dances which would then be combined with the Original Dance rhythm designated by the rules of that season. It would be renamed the Short Dance (SD) and the section would be completed by the existing Free Dance (FD). If successful, this would satisfy the rules required by the IOC and yet preserve the integrity of our sport.

Not the easiest of briefs! It took two years of meetings with coaches, judges, referees, and skaters from all over the world and much heated argument to resolve the many different but equally fervent opinions into a mutually satisfactory conclusion. So I was very touched when Congress came to their feet after passing the proposal and felt it would take our sport into the twenty-first century alive and well. Indeed, the basic concept is still in use today, albeit with numerous innovations and more new Compulsory Dances added.

Compulsory Dances are the building bricks required to produce a champion ice-dance athlete. I liken them to a musician seeking to create a superb overture – an impossible task if they had not mastered the scales on their chosen instrument. They began to appear after the Second World War together with a series of proficiency tests to enable the standard to go on rising. From the Forties to the latter Seventies, these tests were the arbiter by which dancers' abilities were judged, and helped to hone the high standards which won British ice dancers such high esteem throughout the world. Under the aegis of the 'Father of Ice Dance,' Reginald Wilkie, and the members of his national committee, grades of Preliminary, Bronze, Inter-Silver, Silver, and Gold were developed. Later, an Inter-Gold Test was inserted before the final Gold Medal, a standard which very few dancers reached annually, so when one was about to be attempted it always attracted a large audience.

(In 1984, following Torvill and Dean's international successes, an even higher ice dance medal was introduced - the Gold Star, which was skated as a pair, not separately. A very high-level test of any dancer's ability, the test took quite a long time to complete. On the day Chris and Jayne skated it there was a very eminent panel and a very large and enthusiastic audience in their home rink, Nottingham ice Stadium, as well as TV cameras. They were, of course, successful; but to date, no other couple have attempted such a difficult enterprise and they remain the sole holders of this extremely hard-won award).

For the top tests, candidates were required to practice twelve dances. For Silver and Gold tests, the four compulsory dances were drawn the night before to be skated, without any further practice, in the test proper. The Tango, American Waltz, Rocker Foxtrot and Kilian might be selected for Silver tests, while Gold test dances might be four of the following: Viennese Waltz, Gregory Rhumba, Argentine Tango, Quickstep or European Waltz, either clockwise or anti clockwise. (Yes, the European Waltz was considered, despite its simple structure, to be a difficult dance to control and showed the candidate's ability to do so, with good carriage and deportment). For candidates successful so far, these four Compulsory Dances would then be followed, without a break, by the three-minute Free Dance.

To give you some examples, for the 1956 British Ice Dance Championships, one compulsory dance was drawn from each of these groups at 6 pm the night before:

Group 1: Rocker Foxtrot, Foxtrot, Blues
Group 2: European Waltz, American Waltz, Westminster Waltz, Viennese Waltz
Group 3: Kilian, Fourteen Step, Paso Doble, Quickstep
Group 4: The Tango, Argentine Tango, Rhumba.

When June and I competed in the 1958 World Championships in Paris, we were required to skate the Foxtrot, Viennese Waltz, Paso Doble and Tango; in 1959, when Doreen and I competed in Colorado Springs, USA, we skated the Fourteen Step, European Waltz, Paso Doble and Argentine Tango; and in 1960 in Vancouver, we skated the Foxtrot, Viennese Waltz, Quickstep and Tango, in all cases followed by our Free Dance. Quite different to a present-day championship - *Tempus Fugit*!

During my lifetime connection with our sport, I've attended innumerable events. Watching as well as judging these has given me some insights into what constitutes an interesting and successful programme, and I'll share them in the hope that they might be of use in your own connection with our wonderfully artistic sport.

I suggest that creating a routine on ice is much like writing a novel – a thriller! Your music and opening pose are the introduction, an indication of what's to come to whet the appetite of your audience. Within seconds, the opening chapter, your first moves, should be exciting, unexpected and dramatic. You then flow into your story of moves, spins and lifts, with many an unusual twist and turn to maintain interest, making the spectators hold their breath and look forward to the finale towards which your whole presentation is building - in effect, a surprising, dramatic revelation of 'whodunnit.' Remember to include your manner of exit too – the thriller isn't over until you shut the book by actually leaving the ice.

When creating a Free Dance, Rhythm Dance or exhibition

number, the next most important element after your choice of music is the costume you wear to interpret it. Your desired 'look' must be safe and functional to skate in as well as making a striking visual statement to onlookers both near and far.

Over the many years I've been designing skating clothes, I've found numerous special points to consider, so here are my top ten tips for budding champions and those who design and create their costumes:

1. If possible, do your final fitting at the rink under the houselights rather than at home, so that you can view it from a distance as the judges and audience will see it.

2. Try skating in it as part of the fitting process to see how it flows as you perform.

3. Remember that fabrics change colour under different lights. Be very careful when you choose the basic colour, (viewing swatches under rink lighting conditions may help).

4. Small fiddly details and embroidery will only be seen by the judging panel and the front row, certainly not by the back row of a ten thousand-seater stadium! Nonetheless, be creative with your decoration and make it an important part of the outfit. Make it live. Make it **BOLD**.

5. If you use feathers, make sure every frond is stitched securely to the base so that it won't fall off while you're performing and create a hazard for other skaters.

6. Remember ice isn't white but off-white or shades of grey – which makes white outfits, especially using shiny fabrics, hard to design. It's often better to use subtle shades of cream and other soft colours to create your desired effect.

7. When using chiffon, choose silk rather than artificial fibre. Pure silk 'lifts' better in movement and flows well as air passes beneath. It can be hand-dyed to give a graduated effect, and finely pleated chiffon gives a

particularly interesting slant to an outfit.

8. Flesh-coloured fabric is a godsend, because from a distance it does what it's supposed to do, and all sorts of wonderful outfits can be designed using it. However, don't go mad with too much of a nude look; it's figure skating, not an audition for the Follies, so make everything you wear tasteful and suitable for the global family audience who will see you on TV.

9. Ladies: make sure your knickers are decent! A broad, opaque gusset is essential; and if properly cut, your outfit once on should need no adjustment. The same goes for gentlemen: think of your undergarment and make sure it's not too obvious.

10. Remember you're not on a stage being viewed mainly from the front. Skating is theatre in the round, so your costume must look equally good from all angles.

To this fantasy creation must be added your own skating ability, so always try new things and movements which will enhance your performance but are not beyond your skill level. Aspire to technical brilliance and get to know the rules inside out, even better than your coach knows them, to create routines that will pass the test in every respect

This is where things become difficult! Remember to choreograph your performance from the moment you leave the dressing room. With so many cameras around you never know when they will focus on you – so whether you're performing solo or with a partner, remember you are STARS, keep any tantrums private, and enter the arena with smiles on your faces even if you're not speaking to each other or feeling at your best.

The ice arena is your theatre of dreams, and how you occupy the warm-up period is also very, very important. The show has started – you're on! If you feel nervous, don't show it – 'fake it till you make it' and act confident. Talk to each other, connect with your audience by smiles and a pleasant demeanour, (don't forget the judges!), and skate a few easy moves. I suggest you don't do your best moves and lifts during warm-up - save them to wow the audience later. The judges have already seen them in your practice sessions, and if you can't do the moves properly by this time, you have a serious problem! Use the warm-up for exactly that purpose: get your blood flowing, loosen your muscles, calm your nerves, and start getting to know your audience personally.

Your opening stance and first ten seconds of your actual performance are then of paramount importance in establishing the tone of the next crucial three to four minutes. I've seen skaters take a lacklustre pose then skate round the ice rather aimlessly to 'set the whole tone.' Rubbish! The tone should be set by the first bars of your music, your costume and opening stance, and you should aim to have the audience in the palm of your hand within the first ten seconds. To win an Olympic Gold medal you have exactly two hundred and fifty of those to skate your Free Dance, so you can't afford to waste a single one; every precious second must count towards your purpose of *winning*.

It takes brilliant skating to successfully pull off a performance that starts and ends on a slow, quiet note – but of course this has been achieved on numerous occasions which have gone down in skating history. The rhythm of your routine should rise and fall, with light and shade in the choreography, and try to end with something people will remember: a really unusual lift, or music to get the paying public on their feet. I emphasise entertaining the audience because if you succeed in doing so, the judges will be impressed and hopefully reflect that in their final marks.

It's also important, when competing at a high level, to have an alternative idea on hand in case the first doesn't work out when you've skated it a couple of times. Be astute enough to recognise this and make the necessary changes, for instance using the same moves and lifts to a different choice of music, or in a different order.

Remember: a brilliant performance isn't truly achieved until the end of the season. A good skating routine is like a beautiful rose, growing until it blossoms into perfection – but only when it's well pruned.

John Curry and Pat Dodd in 1970 with their British Championship trophies and (centre) Arnold Gerschwiler, by R. Silvester for the NSA, from the BIS Archives

Chapter 13: Golden Boys: Curry and Cousins

Skaters are actors without words who create images on ice, using the ice as a blank canvas on which to paint their creations

My story wouldn't be complete without paying tribute to some of the great British skaters – indeed, some of the world's all-time great ice champions - I had the privilege to be involved with and the pleasure to call friends during my post-competition career.

To begin with the late lamented John Curry, OBE: I'm indebted to Keith Money's brilliant biography for reminding me of dates and events I'd forgotten after so many years.

Born in 1949, John had been taught to skate by Ken Vickers at his local Summerhill Rink in Birmingham since he first took to the ice. I met him at the age of eleven or twelve, when he won what must have been one of his earliest competitions at Queens Ice Club, and I was invited to present his memento. It turned out to be an umbrella, (don't ask why, because I don't know!), and I recall mentioning to someone that the boy had a great future ahead, though it took a few more years for him to really make his mark.

John's early career was marred by the tragic death of his father when he was aged only sixteen, but his mother remained a rock throughout, always supporting his endeavours; we remained in touch after her son's untimely death until she herself died a couple of years ago at the grand age of over one hundred, never losing her humour and determination till the end. A remarkable woman, she enabled her highly gifted youngest son to train with Armand Perren and later with Arnold Gerschwiler, who coached John to his first British title in 1971.

As a troubled genius, John can't have been an easy pupil. He wanted to completely revolutionise the art of free skating, adopting a much more balletic approach and emphasising the importance of choosing the right music to express his expertise. (Simultaneously, across the Atlantic, the late Canadian skater Toller Cranston was trying to achieve something similar; both he and John were finally able to realise their shared hopes and dreams). This resulted in various clashes with various teachers, and John always returned to his close friend and coach Allison Smith for solace and advice; she obviously understood him better than many of his colleagues and remained a mainstay throughout his life.

In 1972, thanks to an American sponsor, John was able to raise the funds to study in the USA with Carlo Fassi and Gus Lussi; the latter taught at Lake Placid, New York, and was renowned for his unusual method of teaching jumps. Alongside the main rink there was a much smaller ice surface, rather like the small Arosa Rink in the old Richmond Ice Rink, which forced skaters to rely on muscular effort to jump rather than relying on the impetus given by skating round a larger rink. John found this very difficult at first, but finally mastered the technique and made extensive use of it thereafter.

While in New York, John met and stayed with a couple who would be his friends and mentors for the rest of his life, Frank and Nancy Streeter. He was beginning to strike lucky - then the cash ran out and he had to return to the UK and to Allison.

Frustrated alike by the inability of his teachers and the skating world in general to accept his inborn balletic style and his efforts to change the way men were 'expected' to skate, he became very depressed and, short of funds, took menial jobs to exist. Confused and unhappy, John was on the verge of giving up. However, by then he was making an impression on the international skating scene as British Champion and a member of the British International Team – and suddenly, someone who had seen him skate in the 1972 European Championships entered the picture.

Ed Mosler, chairman of the fund-raising section of the United States Olympic Committee, recognised the latent genius in John's skating; and for pure love of the sport and a desire to nurture that genius, offered to help him. In one fateful stroke, John's financial troubles were over. He was free to follow the path he had always wanted, and more importantly, to work and create on the ice in the way he wanted, incorporating moves from classical ballet and modern dance.

After many discussions it was decided that he would return to the States to train at the skating school run by Carlo and Crista Fassi, two of the best known and most successful coaches in the world. Apparently, the trio didn't hit it off at first and tensions were felt. It must have been strange for John, moving to a completely new environment with a new group of skaters, most of whom weren't in tune with his ideas as they were so different to those in vogue at the time, and he had to endure some sniggering and crass remarks about his style, which was completely at odds with their overtly masculine routines. Taking no notice, John made them all look foolish in due course.

Luckily, it didn't take him long to realise that Crista and Carlo could help him attain the style, figures, jumps and spins he needed to win, and they soon became lifelong friends as he finally began to achieve the kind of performances he'd dreamed of presenting to the panel of judges. Ed Mosler also became a guardian angel and close friend, responsible for helping this brilliant skater to win Olympic Gold and worldwide fame, and we should all be grateful for Ed's part in creating one of the greatest figure skaters of all time.

In the past, John had often been criticised by judges for the simplicity of his costumes and told that he should add sequins and colour like the other male skaters. He continued to refuse and now, reaching the peak of his career, was able to wear the unadorned costumes he preferred and allow his skating and music to tell the story.

His rise to that elusive Olympic Gold Medal wasn't easy and his performance was somewhat erratic; sometimes he skated well and won a medal, while in other championships he failed to reach the podium. Finally, he participated in the 1976 European Championships in Geneva, Switzerland, (the first championship of the Olympic season – whoever won it would almost certainly be the winner of the Winter Olympics, so a great deal depended on it). At the last free skating session John was in an excellent position to claim the prize, but because of the judging system in place at that time, he had to win the vote of five judges, a majority on the panel of nine. It was rumoured all around the rink that the Soviet bloc, that is the Eastern European countries under Soviet control, were determined that this would not happen.

John knew this as he presented his soon-to-be world-famous Don Quixote routine. He told me that once he'd chosen his music, he put the choreography together within half an hour; he could see the whole thing in his mind's eye, and simply transferred it to ice, giving each individual section a name such as 'Falling Leaf,' and could describe it all in words as well as skating. Understandably, he was very nervous, but skated superbly in a performance described by one American TV commentator as, "one of the finest and most beautiful moments of skating I've ever seen" – and to his amazement, he won!

Later he found out why: the Czech judge was so enthralled that he broke ranks, placed John first, and by doing so made him the Champion of Europe. (On a subsequent visit to Czechoslovakia, a man came up to him and admitted that he was the judge who had changed his mind, and John's fate. No doubt he was thanked profusely!

When it came to the 1976 Winter Olympics in Innsbruck, Austria, John wasn't nervous; his confidence immensely buoyed by being asked to carry the Union flag when the British team entered the arena at the opening ceremony, he knew he was going to win Gold – and he did.

The rest, as they say, is history. Soon afterwards, the World Championships were due to be held in Göteborg, Sweden, and everyone advised him not to compete, saying that he had no need to as his future and fortune were now made. Why put himself through additional trauma? John, being John, wouldn't listen. He was determined to claim the Triple Crown come what may, and in doing so, became the first male skater in the history of our sport to achieve the feat. Invited to join the European exhibition tour with the rest of the skaters, (the usual end to the season), he wasn't keen but capitulated in the end. Naturally, John was extremely nervous skating in the final venue in the USSR, then amazed and elated to have the huge audience on its feet; he even performed an unscripted encore, ending his amateur career with a bang by skating at midnight in

Moscow – a suitably poetic end to the fairy-tale!

On his triumphant return to the UK, John received many honours including an OBE invested by Her Majesty the Queen aboard the Royal Yacht when it was moored in New York Harbour, and the BBC Sports Personality of the Year award for 1976 – the first figure skater ever to receive it. (He was later followed by Robin Cousins, MBE, who also became a household name and helped to further raise our sport's profile by emulating John's Olympic Gold achievement in Lake Placid, New York, in 1980; and four years later by Christopher Dean and Jayne Torvill, who famously won their Gold Medal at the 1984 Winter Olympics in Sarajevo, then in Yugoslavia).

Suddenly, the world was at John Curry's feet, the beautiful bird liberated from his cage to fly wherever he wanted, with the fame, money, and ability to create a completely new art form on ice – which is exactly what he did, at which point I'll let Bobby take up the tale:

'I had known of and admired John throughout his skating career, but it wasn't until I became a coach and was watching him train at Richmond Ice Rink, under the tutelage of Allison Smith, that we would pass the time of day and I really became in awe of his undoubted talent.

Then when I was coaching members of the International British Ice Dance Team, we chatted more, and I got to know him better. We established a rapport that was to extend throughout his life, and I felt very honoured that he would turn to me to discuss his hopes and dreams; we appeared to be on the same wavelength, his friendship began to mean a great deal to me, and I, in turn, learnt a great deal from him. Courtney and he also had an affinity; both were anxious to widen the scope of their respective disciplines with new music and ideas that weren't always popular with the judging elites in control of our sports, and who were greatly opposed to such changes. All of us worked separately and together, in our own ways, to achieve a completely new approach to competitive skating, which often proved to be an uphill struggle.

John experienced and overcame many hardships along the

way, adding to his wonderful talent on ice a great acting ability, creative choreography, and an uncontrolled zest for a change of direction in the way male skaters presented their routines.

During a practice session for the 1976 Winter Olympics, we were discussing how he might improve his 'Don Quixote' routine and I suggested that, as he finished the performance with one knee on the ice, he should stay in position to milk the tumultuous applause I knew he'd receive, rather than rising immediately.

John agreed to try this. I'd been at the event coaching British Team members Kay Barsdell and Kenneth Foster but wasn't allowed to remain in the Olympic Village after the Ice Dance event was complete, because the accommodation was required for the incoming coaches of later events. So I had to return to the UK before John skated in the Men's final; and two days later, when we were sitting at home mesmerised, like millions of others, by his wonderful win and presentation on the podium, the telephone suddenly rang.

I answered it. A voice said, "Hullo, Bobby – it's John."

I immediately shouted, "Congratulations!"

He replied by asking what I'd thought of his performance, and whether he'd stayed on one knee long enough at the end.

"John," I exploded, "You've just won an Olympic Gold Medal! Why do you want my opinion?"

"Because your opinion is very important to me," he replied. I was speechless, and it's a moment I'll never forget. John was also kind enough to refer to me as his mentor, which I consider a huge honour.

After John turned professional and had his own show on Broadway, we were both in New York; he was preparing a new show, and I was coaching Judy Blumberg and Michael Siebert, the American Ice Dance Champions, for the 1984 Winter Olympic Games.

I wasn't at all popular with the American sports press, who couldn't understand why any of their sportsmen or women would even consider being trained by a coach who wasn't American – the idea was anathema to them. Consequently, I was ostracised to a certain extent by the press and the US coaching fraternity, but Judy and Michael gave me wonderful introductions to the American Ballet Theatre and the very famous ballerina Georgina Parkinson, who became a dear friend, along with many other dancers who helped me mould Judy and Michael's incredible talent. Not only that, through these people I was able to widen my knowledge in a way that wouldn't have been possible without Judy and Michael's help. I learnt such a lot during this period.

After I returned to the UK, John rang again to say that he had an audition that afternoon with Agnes de Mille, the famous producer, for a singing lead in the Broadway version of *Brigadoon*, and he was very nervous. I promised him that his talent would win out and sure enough, it did – the show played on Broadway for many months, with John in one of the lead roles as a villain.

By then, his talent off the ice as well as on was really beginning to show. Already an excellent actor, he had toured the USA in a play, and produced a show on TV where he skated between musicians of the Philharmonic Orchestra seated on the ice. Back in London, he appeared in Shakespeare in Regent's Park, and played six different characters in a Charles Dickens presentation at the King's Head Pub Theatre in Islington. An all-round talent, he also danced on stage with Anthony Dowell, and had hugely successful shows at the Palladium Theatre in the West End and at the Royal Albert Hall.

Courtney and I both remained friends with John until his untimely death in 1995, aged only forty-four, with so much left still to offer. His life and amazing talent left a lasting mark on the world of entertainment, and his huge influence on the world of skating is felt even today.

Chloe Ronaldson, the *Guinness Book of Records* holder of many roller speed skating world titles and a friend to all three of us, decided that his passing should be marked by his myriad of friends and admirers, and organized a memorial celebration in a hall in Red Lion Square in the West End. There were readings, dancing, and words by many stars of stage and ice, many laughs and some tears. It was a great privilege for me to speak at this gathering, although I found it very difficult to put into words my feelings about his life, they were so varied. In the end I simply spoke about his tremendous talents as meaningfully as I could, (Millicent Martin came up later and congratulated me, so perhaps I did a reasonable job), and we all agreed that the party turned out to be a very suitable celebration of John's life.

His legacy both on and off the ice lives on.'

Robin Cousins, MBE, the second of my skating greats, followed in John Curry's illustrious footsteps just a few years later. Robin already had a sporting connection, his father Fred had been an apprentice goalkeeper for Millwall Football Club before the war, but his own sporting career began, by a strange coincidence, in the same way as mine: he fell in love with ice skating when he first set foot on it, as I had done, at the Westover Ice Rink in Bournemouth. I was four years old when I began skating in 1937, and Robin was six, on holiday in Bournemouth with his parents and older brothers, Martin and Nick, in 1963.

In Robin's own words, quoted from our personal correspondence by his kind permission:

'Yes, the glamorous Bournemouth Ice Follies! It was their colourful poster, reminiscent of a Hollywood/Vegas show, that drew me to the window - and then seeing inside where these people were whizzing around on a public session. I was mesmerised. I don't remember much of the skating I tried for the first time, but I know I was hooked immediately! One of the coaches told my mother about the ice rink being built in Bristol, (my hometown), and I think it was a year after the rink was open that I asked for skating lessons as a Christmas present. That Christmas present was Pamela Davies, [not the skating judge] who took my 'Learn to Skate' class and then coached me right through to my first World Championship.'

So began Robin's incredible journey to Olympic Gold and worldwide acclaim, not only on ice but also on the stage and screen. After training with my good friend Pam Davies, his special ability was soon recognised; having virtually seen him grow up into manhood, it was obvious to me that he was essentially a figure skater who was also at heart an ice dancer. Robin also possessed additional talents like being able to spin in both directions - a kind of ambidextrous skater, so to speak, who also mastered the Back Flip, (I wonder how judges in the top skating events would have reacted if he had included one in his famous competition routines!).

Accepted as a pupil by Gladys Hogg, Robin relocated to London to train at Queens Ice Club. Like a true champion, he showed his commitment and determination by stacking shelves at Whitley's Department Store in Queensway to help pay for his lessons and travel home on the weekends. As he was Pam's pupil, I naturally followed his progress with interest:

'Back in the day,' Robin goes on, 'you didn't meet or converse with judges or officials unless they came to you (or the coach) at competitions. It certainly felt when I was very early in my career, that there was an air of the judges being 'gods' who would deign to acknowledge your performance. I know as an ice dancer my coach Pamela Davies knew Courtney via her former coach and skating partner. [At} a lot of the early competitions for me the dance and figure skating were quite separate, so I can't point to a specific event or date [when I first met Courtney, although as] one of the only former world champions who had a presence both within our national governing body and the ISU, (Haig Oundjian would do likewise in the Nineties), he was very influential. Our paths crossed more when I became a senior and started competing internationally.'

Finally, like so many of our skaters, Robin moved to the USA to become a pupil of Carlo Fassi, who honed his skills to the high standard required to be world class.

'As you know and experienced, Gladys [Hogg] never flew anywhere, so unless she could take a train she didn't go to competitions. My first World Championships were to be in the USA, at the Broadmoor in Colorado Springs in 1975. My first Worlds, (I had withdrawn the year before due to my first knee injury during the official practice), and no coach. Gladys had arranged for me to be looked after by her old skating partner, Ronnie Baker, whilst I was there, (along with Janet Thompson and Warren Maxwell). I can't say I remember much of anything of Ronnie from that experience, but what I do know is that a very fun and feisty British lady introduced herself to me. Once met, never to forget - the force that is Doreen Denny. Suffice to say, once I was part of Carlo Fassi's training camp in Denver there would be frequent visits to the Broadmoor for galas

Robin Cousins by Fred Dean, courtesy of Paul Dean.

and competitions and I always tried to get my Doreen fix. She was so supportive and encouraging - and of course, there were stories. I think she may have 'wound' you and Gladys up just a little!? It's making me smile just writing this,' says Robin.

I watched Robin's progress as he went on to represent Great Britain for eight seasons, moving higher and higher up the ladder and finally crowning his early career by winning the Gold Medal at the 1980 Winter Olympics in Lake Placid, New York. He became BBC Sports Personality of the Year the same year, and then skated into a new career as a consummate professional after retiring from the amateur ranks.

Many of his colleagues would have then moved into lucrative coaching for the rest of their lives. Robin wasn't one of those skaters! He immediately diversified into new creative projects and showed what varied talents he possesses as an all-round entertainer. His excellent singing voice netted him parts in shows like Rogers & Hammerstein's *Cinderella*, Andrew Lloyd-Webber's *Cats*, and Richard O'Brien's *Rocky Horror Show*, along with an invitation to perform at the concert preceding the 1995 World Figure Skating Championships at Birmingham's NEC. A very successful choreographer too, Robin has created for competitive skaters, touring ice shows and television specials, all this whilst becoming a very knowledgeable and highly respected commentator for worldwide championships and the Winter Olympics. His successes are too long and varied to list here, and serve as a lesson to today's young skaters: not only must you learn to skate if you aspire to be a champion, but you should also enhance other talents off the ice if you aspire to become a figure skating icon like Robin Cousins. Dancing, acting, body control, and a love of music - these and other qualities need to be added to a natural ability to skate to the highest standard.

Recognised by the award of an MBE in the Queen's 1980 New Year's Honours List, and currently President of British Ice Skating, as our sport's governing body is now known, Robin continues to use his knowledge and talents to help young skaters all over the country to reach their goals. There could be no better mentor, and I shall give him the last word:

'I am very grateful for the time you took, over the course of my own career, to always give me your thoughts and advice. You took the time to articulate, it was never disapproving, just honest and forthright. I don't suppose any skater truly appreciates this until much later, but I seem to recall you took interest in me, (and Pam), very early on in my career. Maybe the connection to my being taught the basics so well by an ice dancer helped!? She certainly held you in high esteem and ALWAYS taught us singles skaters with an ice dancer's eye. I'm not complaining!

I suppose the past year has given many people time to reflect, re-evaluate and be so grateful for what we've had, what we've been given and what we can look forward to. I feel lucky to have my 'white canvas of ice' very much still part of my life and I hope that won't change anytime soon. Maybe it's more in a glass with gin than underfoot currently, but with the rinks opening up and competitions being scheduled let's keep our fingers crossed that more youngsters will have the opportunity to experience in their future what you and I have been fortunate to have in our past.'

Chapter 14: Our Last Golden Couple: Torvill and Dean

Music is the vocabulary of skating

In the late Seventies, a very unworldly but hugely talented couple, Christopher Dean and Jayne Torvill, entered our lives and are still part of it over forty years later.

At that time, they were being trained by Janet Sawbridge at the Nottingham Ice Stadium and beginning to show great promise. However, Janet had decided to retire, and they were searching for a replacement; having been advised by some of the judging panel to ask Betty Callaway to take over, this was about to happen.

Mrs Vera Pilsworth had also been keeping a motherly eye on the couple, as she and her family were Directors of the Board that ran the Stadium, and Chris and Jayne spent a great deal of their free time in their home. Vera approached Bobby and me during a visit to Nottingham and asked whether we would help Chris and Jayne by suggesting some ideas for their skating costumes as they began to enter the international scene. It was the inauspicious start of a friendship that has lasted ever since, and they have risen from a rather shy but talented pair of unknowns to the household names they are today.

Naturally, when we were discussing costumes and 'makeover' Bobby joined in, and the four of us began to informally discuss their skating and choice of music with Betty. (Betty already had a successful international career, teaching skaters from various countries; she was a highly technical exponent and very knowledgeable about the skating politics of countries now entering the field of ice dancing). We like to think that we all worked well together, and our rather unusual approach to music, costume and choreography added an extra layer to the mix and began to produce a couple who will live on forever in the annals of our sport.

Later, I was very honoured to be the British Judge for the Ice

Dance event at the 1984 Olympic Winter Games, and my heart was in my mouth as Chris and Jayne skated 'Bolero,' knowing all the pitfalls that could occur; but luckily, I was able to show two perfect sixes when the scores appeared all over the world. As an amateur, I've always considered judging these large international events a great personal responsibility, because when you raise your respective marks for a skater's performance, you're literally holding their financial future and the rest of their lives in your hands... and you'll soon understand our belief in their talent and why Chris and Jayne figure so many times in the narrative you've been reading.

In 1981, Christopher and Jayne won their first World Championship title in Hartford, USA, and their amazing career really began to take off. Their win was well-deserved but unexpected: Judy Blumberg and Michael Seibert were the current US National Champions, and favourites to win as they too were bringing a completely new approach into the Original Dance and Free Dance. The Russian contingent was also very strong indeed and expected to be on the podium. Then one after another, the dancers in the last group to take the ice made errors they would never have made under normal circumstances, while Chris and Jayne, perhaps with British grit, skated their usual best and stormed to victory - a title neither they nor the audience had ever expected them to win, as in 1979 they had finished in eighth place rather than on the podium.

With this win they began to prove what great ice dancers they were, and to take the place they richly deserve in the history of our sport. 1982 dawned with Chris and Jayne as the new World Champions, having broken the hold of the Russian, and more recently Hungarian, domination of international ice dancing, (begun after 1970, when Diane Towler and Bernard Ford retired having taken the World and European crowns for the past four years). These skaters had completely changed the face of ice dancing by introducing different musical choices and a much faster way of skating in their innovative free dance routines. Ludmila Pakhomova and Alexandr Gorshkov, who would go on to win six World Championship Gold Medals from 1970, crowned by their success in winning the USSR's first ever Olympic Gold Medal in 1976 with their dance-orientated approach based on Russian ballet and music, using Russian choreographers and costume designers. They and their compatriots who followed made, and are still making, a huge contribution to the discipline; but in 1982, Torvill and Dean were determined to change the Ice Dance event once more, and a legend was about to be born.

For Chris and Jayne, their Original Dance and Free Dance for the 1982 European and World Championships were therefore of paramount importance in establishing their superiority, so they had to start planning both at an early stage, as well as continuing to excel at the Compulsory Dances.

In the late summer of 1981, we all happened to be in Morzine, France, where Chris and Jayne were present for an event. As usual, with their incredible work ethic, they were already in deep discussions about their choice of music for the next season's championships, (they always planned twelve months ahead). They were determined, as ever, to create something entirely new with their music, and as we sat in their room, they played one CD after another. Then suddenly Chris put on a short burst of a new hit musical being staged on Broadway, *Mack and Mabel* written by Jerry Herman. 'The musical was first performed in 1974 but wasn't a success,' says Chris. 'We found the music in the BBC Nottingham radio library and first listened to it in 1980. We felt it wasn't right for us then, but after the 1981 Worlds, it came onto our radar again and we knew it was perfect for us going forward.' We all agreed that we liked this best of all, which nonplussed Chris as he had no idea how to obtain a complete version of the musical, there being no recordings available at that time in the U.K. Anyway, he managed to get the full version sent over, and as soon as it arrived, we all knew this was 'It'.

The costumes had to be as innovative and showy as the music. Sitting in the bedroom in Morzine, we started visualising how to create the dance while I sketched, on an old brown envelope, (the only paper available). These sketches became what the late critic and journalist Clive James dubbed in a newspaper column the 'Gold Fag Packet' outfits.

They took the envelope back to Richmond, and Mrs Sylvia

Parrish created the dress that Jayne would wear. Because it had a skirt trimmed with ostrich feathers and there was a fear they could moult and endanger the skaters, she sewed each individual frond of the feathers on individually - a definite labour of love! Meanwhile Chris took my sketch of his suit to a tailor who made a matching gold suit that perfectly complemented Jayne's dress.

The resulting 'Mack and Mabel' Free Dance routine, with the combination of their brilliant skating, choreography, music, and costume, all relating to and enhancing each other, really broke the mould and set the bar for ice dancing even higher.

This standard continued to rise with the next routine they conceived during the winter of 1981 – 82. Chris and Jayne were in Russia, and on a free evening their hosts offered them a ticket to the ballet and one for the circus. Jayne had always loved ballet and opted for that, so Chris went to the circus, which in Russia is very special and greatly loved. Chris had never seen anything like it and came back full of excitement about its colour and brilliance – so there and then, the concept of their next Free Dance was decided.

When they returned to the UK, we started discussing it over a meal. Chris and Jayne were bubbling over with ideas, and it so happened that Michael Crawford was currently wowing audiences at the London Palladium with his great musical extravaganza *Barnum*. They thought seeing the show would be a great way to start their planning, and kindly invited us to join them.

Once seated, Chris and Jayne created quite a stir when the audience realised that they were there, and people were climbing over seats to capture their autographs. Unbeknown to us, Michael Crawford, wondering what was causing the commotion, looked through a spy hole on stage and invited us to join him in his dressing room after the show. He was absolutely charming, and when Jayne and Chris explained the reason for the visit he offered to help, and spent many hours over the next few months at the ice sessions as well as advising them on all the circus movements they were planning to use in their new routine. Chris was to become, in effect, the Ringmaster, and Jayne the Trapeze Artist, as the choreography suggests in the slow piece. Their movements were to include the clowns, the tightrope walker and other circus acts - quite a daunting idea.

The whole routine began to take shape on the ice at Peterborough Ice Rink. It wasn't easy, but the music spoke for itself, and Chris and Jayne worked hard to interpret this exciting project. No other couple had ever succeeded in bringing the circus to the ice in a competition routine remaining within the strict guidelines laid down for Championships, yet with all the required elements being included.

The music could be reduced into a four-minute programme, and it was amazing how the musicians managed to achieve such a magical effect lasting for such a relatively short time; in a first for the couple, conductor Michael Reed orchestrated a bespoke Overture for which all the musicians donated their time. Designing the costumes was great fun too and we decided, once more, to deviate by dressing basically in white, which was considered very unusual in those days. It had to be completely different from their Mack and Mabel outfits, but epitomise show business in a style appropriate for a competitive routine. Chris was to be very dominant as the Ringmaster, who would normally wear a red tailcoat, and Jayne's costume would be a pleated version of a ballet skirt using only two colours – white, with turquoise satin trim. Once again, Sylvia Parrish made an excellent job of creating the costumes, and the result was something absolutely new to present to the judging panel.

Michael Crawford was a tower of strength during the creation of the routine and was often at the rink offering endless helpful comments. 'Mack and Mabel' was a hard act to follow, but 'Barnum & Bailey' was a triumph of co-ordinating a showbiz effect with the fluidity and difficulty of skating to the same rules all competitors must obey. Unfortunately, due to Jayne suffering a shoulder injury, they had to miss the 1983 European Championships, which piled on the pressure when it came to the Worlds in Helsinki, Finland – where, yet again, Torvill and Dean demonstrated their incredible skating ability as well as creating something quite new, and took a well-deserved Gold Medal.

Their lasting contribution to the discipline of ice dancing

Above: Preparing Barnum with (left to right) me, Michael Crawford, Betty Callaway, Christopher Dean, Jayne Torvill

Below: Jayne and Chris after Barnum, reproduced from Ice and Roller Skate, *courtesy of Paul Dean*

would be illustrated once more when they set their sights on Olympic Gold. Their brilliant skating and choreography had won them both European and World crowns, but even then, plans were being discussed for the all-important Olympic year, 1984

For the Olympics, the musical choice, style and creation of the Original Dance, (which had to be skated to a Paso Doble rhythm), was of paramount importance. Chris and Jayne spent countless hours discussing how they were to skate a dance that would be completely different and more memorable than those presented by their rivals – which was no easy task, as the standard of the competition rose every season. After long discussion with everyone concerned, they finally decided on a very unusual version of *Cappricio Espanole* with many highs and lows in the composition and a dramatic finale which, when they skated it, would bring the audience to their feet. The whole dance was to express the matador, preening himself whilst tempting the bull before the final kill. Again, it was to be very different in its choice of music and composition, whilst still adhering to the complicated rules. That was the difficult part. In one sequence, Chris, the proud Matador, would drag his cape while strutting in defiance of the bull. Bobby helped him master the move and suggested that he tried to conquer it on the floor before trying it on the ice. Chris had his doubts as to how that would work and spent many hours trying to perfect the movement, destined to be the one most photographed by the press - an iconic image of immaculate skating, and famous worldwide.

When we discussed the design of their outfits, we agreed to discard the normal expectation of black and red, deciding instead on black and white. Jayne's dress would express the cape, and I designed it to be black on one side and white on the other so that the picture they were creating on the ice would constantly change, depending on which view the audience saw. The dress had very heavy bands of embroidery from the neck down the arm to the wrist, a deliberate addition attached to an unseen underdress; at one stage in the dance, Chris drops Jayne virtually to ice level in one fast movement, then immediately brings her back up again without touching the ice. The costume weighed about twelve pounds, with the extra weight of the embroidery helping to take Jayne down even faster, and we used a washable polyester throughout because she ended up flat on the ice, so it had to be sponge-able and quick drying - basically, an elegant drip-dry skating dress!

The result was a thrillingly dramatic evocation of a bullfight which would later bring Torvill and Dean another historic string of perfect sixes for interpretation from the judges.

Now thoughts turned to the Free Dance. The most forward planning and forward-looking couple I've ever known, Chris and Jayne had been discussing this almost since the moment they stepped off the ice after their successes of the previous season; and although we didn't know it, that Free Dance, with the music they chose, was destined to become the most famous in history and to this day is shown all over the world.

At that time, we lived in a mews house in Ladbroke Grove, West London, (long before it became fashionable and swept to fame in the film *Notting Hill Gate*), and often the couple would come down to spend a weekend with us, suffer my cooking, listen to music, and make plans. They were able to use practice ice in the Lea Valley Ice Centre, which saved funds for future projects, and we always enjoyed their company and enthusiasm.

On the weekend in question, they arrived with a whole pile of cassettes and CDs, and on Saturday evening we had the usual brainstorming session which often went on well into the night. Chris said that he had quite a few ideas, one of which he thought could well be The One, and after supper went down to the car to get them so we could listen whilst I did the washing up. Bobby and I were in the kitchen when we heard *42nd Street* go on. We looked at each other and said, "No way. It's too much like 'Mack and Mabel' and 'Barnum' - been there, done that. We need something completely different for Olympic year."

Chris's face fell - he was very disheartened because that was the music he'd had in mind. But Jayne said, "They haven't led us wrong yet," and for the next hour or so we listened to endless CDs which were all discarded. Then suddenly Chris put on Ravel's *Bolero*.

Bobby and I both said, "That's it!" – much to Chris's consternation, as they'd only used it for warming up before their practice sessions, and never considered it as a possibility. He added that no couple had ever used the same melody from start to finish in a four-minute competition routine, such an experiment might not work, and the judges might not accept a change in presentation which would seriously move the goalposts for international championship events. This had never been tried before and could be very dangerous - a daunting prospect!

But as we talked and talked through that evening and late into the night, 'Bolero' started coming to life and we all became much more excited about the possibilities, seeing in our minds' eye the excitement building from the throbbing drum beat at the beginning to the incredible climax. (After that we played Bolero so many times over the coming months that our next-door neighbour Jeany Savage, the famous fashion photographer, heard it through the walls so often that she said she felt like she'd skated every step herself!). But what sort of costume would be in keeping with the passionate, sensuous feel of the piece?

For the colour we picked Iris Purple, a favourite of them both, which is very rarely used on ice and therefore in itself an innovation. I started on Christopher's costume – the most difficult to design - that same evening after clearing up the supper things. We decided he would wear a 'New Romantic' loose top with flowing sleeves and minimal decoration, with deep purple trousers. Jayne's dress would complement this in a classical Greek style, simple and flowing, once again with a minimum of decoration. We would use silk chiffon because the air moves it better, as you skate, than a man-made version. However, the dress would be very delicate and had to touch the wet ice as little as possible.

To get the shaded effect I needed we hung the fabric over a bucket of deep purple dye in the basement, (next to the loo, to Chris's lasting amusement), and every time we passed, we raised the fabric a little higher and stirred the dye with the wooden spoon I'd been using to make dinner on the night in question. (As you can see, we still have that spoon as a memento of a very special time in our lives!). That way the fabric became darker at the base and lighter at the top, and we sent it off to Mrs Parrish to make Jayne's final dress and Chris's top.

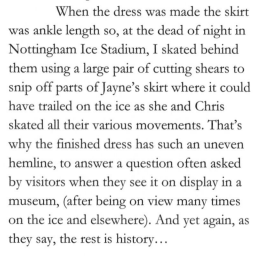

When the dress was made the skirt was ankle length so, at the dead of night in Nottingham Ice Stadium, I skated behind them using a large pair of cutting shears to snip off parts of Jayne's skirt where it could have trailed on the ice as she and Chris skated all their various movements. That's why the finished dress has such an uneven hemline, to answer a question often asked by visitors when they see it on display in a museum, (after being on view many times on the ice and elsewhere). And yet again, as they say, the rest is history…

My own contribution to the 1984 Winter Olympics was designing and co-ordinating the uniforms for the whole Great Britain Team. It was, of course, an unpaid appointment, but I was charged with dealing with clothing firms all over the country and trying to get the hundreds of outfits either free in return for the publicity, or at the lowest cost available.

The project took up a great deal of time but was extremely interesting and I met many people who became lifelong friends. Early on I was lucky enough to be seated, during an official dinner, next to the CEO of Aquascutum, so taking advantage of this, I suggested that his company became involved. He agreed, resulting in a perfect partnership between this quintessentially British company, the NSA and the Winter Olympics that lasted until 1995, when I chaired the

Organising Committee of the ISU World Figure Skating Championships in Birmingham and Aquascutum provided the outfits for the two hundred and fifty wonderful people from all over the UK who helped with the event. Sadly, afterwards the Association took a different course and uniforms are no longer considered necessary for British skaters attending international events all over the world.

When the outfits were being discussed, it was kept under wraps that HRH Princess Royal, then Chair of the British Olympic Association, was to be measured for the official uniform under an assumed name. I was very proud to see Princess Anne wearing it throughout the event, and many years later, delighted to see the white angora ski headdress I had designed, in conjunction with Lillywhites of Piccadilly, being worn by Princess Diana during one of her winter skiing trips. It just goes to show how careful the Royal Family is when it comes to reusing their clothing!

It was also a very proud moment for me to see the large British Team march into the Olympic Stadium wearing the outfits I'd had the great honour of designing. The blazers were so successful they were made again in the same colours and style, but in a lighter weight cloth, by the same company for the next Summer Olympic Games. (I also designed the outfits for the British Swimming Team when they competed in the following year's World Championships).

In 1984, having been World Ice Dance Champions for three years, Chris and Jayne arrived in Hungary to claim the European title for their own, then went on to Sarajevo surrounded by rumours about their revolutionary Free Dance.

The Russians were particularly determined that their dancers should top the podium and had trained to a very high standard using all the best choreographers and costume designers to achieve this end. Out of the nine judges who would judge the event, the balance of power rested with the Eastern Bloc so Chris and Jayne would be hard pressed to win over the whole panel in their favour, especially with the goal of a Gold Olympic Medal in sight and the enormous prestige and monetary returns attached to it.

Due to work commitments, I was unable to attend this event

but was a non-travelling substitute judge for Great Britain. However, the word was that even the British judge would go along with the pack to avoid suspension for National Bias! Chris and Jayne's Free Dance was causing judges' eyebrows to be raised at the pre-event practice sessions because it was such a new approach, and rumour had it that those who considered one of the routine's final lifts to break the rules would take the opportunity to knock a mark off, legitimately – a deduction, at this high standard, which would deprive them of their win and the expected achievement of an Olympic Gold Medal to follow their European title.

The judging of Figure Skating and Ice Dancing has always been an exact science and the judges and referees receive many years of experience and training before they're eligible to judge at championship level. Three decades ago, the rules regarding ice dancing were very precise, with the various movements and lifts governed by strict written rules. Should a judge be found to have deviated from these rules, the referee was empowered to request a written explanation at their official meeting with the panel immediately following the event. If the referee considered that the judge in question had shown national bias or ignored a movement that contravened the rules, thereby placing a competitor in a higher or lower place than the referee considered correct, the case was conveyed to a higher body with the referee's recommendation for a sanction, or dismissal for a certain length of time, before they were reinstated. So, if a judge *did* make a deliberate mistake and therefore possibly faced a disciplinary punishment, he or she had to be very certain of their reasons for doing so.

Nowadays, not only has the quality and physical ability of the skaters advanced light years beyond what it was then, so have the judging regulations. The mathematics involved in being an international judge in all disciplines is very, very complicated and, with the introduction of judging by computer, any errors can be immediately seen by the referee, even before they are shown to the public, and then the breakdown of every skater's mark is immediately available to everyone. Whether this has improved the creativity and choice of music by the skaters is a moot point and the jury is still out!

Nevertheless, we have the benefit of enjoying incredible performances by the competitors skating for us today.

Bobby discussed the potential dire scenario with Chris, Jayne and Betty. They all said the only option was for me to fly over, throw my weight around behind the scenes, and try to think of a way out. The telephones were not exactly private at that time, especially in the hotel. Bobby rang me and spoke in gibberish, over the sound of the bath running, about how they 'needed me.' I managed to decode the message behind the call. Despite the problem of being at work and having to pay for my flight, I had such respect for Chris and Jayne's talent that I talked myself into taking leave and flying to the event, where I would be accredited as the official reserve British judge.

On landing I went immediately to the stadium, asked around and discovered that the rumours were true - even the British judge was going to acquiesce. I told the Referee, Lawrence Demmy. He didn't believe me at first, but a couple of hours later came back and said that although this was indeed the case, as an impartial referee he could do nothing to change the situation.

So later that day we had a council of war! There was no alternative but to change the lift to make it 'legal.' Chris and Jayne said this was impossible as they had skated their last official practice and would only have a very brief one the next morning, then the five-minute warm-up period before they skated their actual Free Dance. We accordingly set about changing the lift, not on the ice but in the hotel room! Every time they said, "It's impossible," we tried again, until late in the evening. I made one suggestion: they shouldn't try it on the ice in the morning session, nor in the warm-up before they skated. If they did, the judges would know what was up and have the chance to reassess their marks.

The next day dawned with fear and trepidation for all of us. What if it went wrong and Chris and Jayne fell trying to execute the new lift? A fall would mean a larger deduction - they might even be off the podium, with all their dreams of Olympic Gold dashed forever.

With me seated in the arena, Betty Callaway at the barrier, and Bobby at ice level as he was coaching four other couples from four different countries, time stopped still for all of us for four minutes and ten seconds. The music began. Slowly, sensuously, they rose from their knees and flowed smoothly into the near-flawless performance destined to become a skating legend. It's an enormous credit to their inborn mastery that they managed pull off, if slightly unsteadily, the lift they had never practised on ice - to the consternation of the whole judging panel, who had no alternative but to accept it as it obeyed every rule to the letter, and award them the Gold Medal. (It's interesting that over three decades later, Ravel is still best known all over the world as the composer of 'Torvill and Dean's music,' and even today, TV adverts use the piece as the background to promote the smoothness and elegance of a product - quite a legacy for any skaters).

However, immediately afterwards it was back to Nottingham to revamp the Free Dance and go through every movement to make sure that everything was completely within the rules laid down at that time and prevent such a hiatus ever recurring! Now a part of skating history, 'Bolero' went on to win the Gold Medal in those forthcoming Olympic Games, and Chris and Jayne found their place in our sport for ever after.

During my working life as a fashion designer, I also enjoyed designing skating outfits as a hobby, (some of which, I'm honoured to say, have ended up in museums). So I was very excited when, after their Olympic triumph, Chris and Jayne turned professional and they invited me to join them as part of their design team when they went to Australia to mount and star in their first lavish ice show.

I duly travelled to Australia for the first time and found designing for a number of skaters to be quite different from designing for individuals; I learnt a great deal and it was a great experience, though I'm not sure this branch of design work was my forte. (I also fell in love with Australia, which I then visited on many more occasions).

While I was there, an unforgettable incident occurred when we and the whole of the cast were given the weekend off and went to relax in a house on the beach for two days. Naturally everyone made for the sea and Chris, who was a very strong swimmer, was first in the water. Jayne and I decided not to swim and instead walked along the beach for an ice cream. On the way back, we saw Chris waving quite a long way out. We waved back. Then Jayne suddenly said, "I think he's in trouble." She was right - he was waving for help! We rushed to raise the alarm and one of the skaters, another strong swimmer, raced into the water and went to his aid.

Regaining his composure, Chris returned to all of us waiting anxiously on the beach... and I can't even bear to consider what might have happened if we hadn't seen him waving.

In 1993, Chris and Jayne paid us a surprise visit in Wesley Square to discuss a very important project they had in mind: after a gap of ten years, they'd decided to return to competition and try to regain the Olympic Crown they had won with 'Bolero.'

Needless to say, we were totally astonished! They were enjoying worldwide success with their skating exhibitions and shows, and to attempt such a monumental project they would first have to regain their amateur status, (which was possible under the rules in force at that time), both nationally and internationally. In the full glare of the popularity they both now enjoyed all over the world, they then would start the arduous process of training for the Compulsory Dances, as well as creating a new Original Dance, following the strict rules of the forthcoming season, to rival and even improve upon their 'Bolero' routine.

By that time both had acquired partners off the ice: Jayne was with Phil Christensen and Chris with Jill Trenary, herself a famous World Figure Skating Champion from the USA. Their partners were equally enthusiastic and agreed to fully support them in their 'comeback' endeavour, even though no other Olympic gold medallists had ever attempted such a feat after such a long interval.

Jayne and Chris then asked Bobby to come on board as their coach. After careful consideration, he advised them it would be better for Betty Callaway to remain as before and name him instead as their joint coach, although he would continue to support all three of them in every way possible. They also asked me to design their costumes once more, which I was more than delighted to do. Their sponsor, a company named Chrisanne, worked on my designs and created them in their excellent workrooms once they had been approved by Chris and Jayne.

It was, for all involved, a very exciting project, but professionally a very dangerous and daunting one. As usual, the pair set about the task with the same dedication and enthusiasm they'd shown a decade earlier. They arranged for ice to be available at Milton Keynes Ice Rink in Buckinghamshire, where they could practice uninterrupted by the public, and started to discuss how to apportion time and ice for each part of this new challenge. Firstly, though, they had to compete in the forthcoming British Ice Dance Championships in Sheffield, South Yorkshire - the first test of their ability to skate once more at competition standard, and within competition constraints. The European Championships in Copenhagen, Denmark, would follow two months later in January 1994, when they would be competing against couples from all over Europe, many of whom would be considerably younger than themselves. All this would be essential preparation for the Winter Olympics which would take place in Norway a few weeks later, and their bid for another Gold Medal.

Jayne and Chris started to train for the three Compulsory Dances, in this case the Starlight Waltz, (which Peri and I had created), Blues, and Tango Romantica, and also to create an Original Dance to the Rumba rhythm, (the rhythm to be used was designated annually), as memorable as their 1984 Paso Doble, plus a Free Dance to equal or surpass Bolero. Not an easy task, especially as there had been major changes during the last decade in the way the discipline was judged internationally. Most importantly, the dissolution of the USSR allowed countries under the former communist umbrella to compete as separate individual members, as they had been before World War Two, thus increasing the number of contestants, judges, and referees who could compete under the flag of their nation, and irrevocably changing the dynamics of the sport and its judging.

Bearing these changes in mind, we had endless round table discussions, but the pair were adamant that they wanted to return to the field of play. Chris and Jayne finally decided to skate to *History of*

Love for the Rumba, and endeavour to create the aura of their idols
Fred Astaire and Ginger Rogers by using *Let's Face the Music and Dance*
for their Free Dance routine, in a nostalgic tribute to their heroes.
Choosing the music was a relatively easy part! Adhering strictly to the
new rules now in force sometimes inhibited their creativity; however,
they were determined to use the rules to their advantage rather than
to their detriment while remaining as creative as they could. Five
different Original Dances were created and discarded over as many
weeks, with many tears of frustration, before the very seductive final
version was approved by their coaches and advisors. (The ISU Ice
Dance Committee recently confirmed that a version of that same
Rumba, known as 'Rumba d'Amor,' will now be skated in their
Championships as a Compulsory Dance, so it will never be
forgotten).

Chris and Jayne travelled to Copenhagen for the European
Championships in the knowledge that, to achieve their Olympic aim,
it was an absolute necessity for them to win this event against fierce
competition. They had always been a contemplative pair, usually
skating very quietly and calmly in the warm-up periods and practice
sessions, so felt somewhat inhibited by other couples flying round the
rink paying little heed to their fellow competitors. As the
Championships proceeded, extremely disappointed by their third
place in the Compulsories, they came back fighting with their special
Rumba, which captivated the judges as well as the audience and got
them back to the top of the pack. Now everything rested on the final
Free Dance section.

With 'Let's Face the Music and Dance,' Torvill and Dean
finally came into their own. In the most closely contested result in the
history of ice dancing, and ten years after their retirement, Chris and
Jayne beat the Russian pairs Grishuk and Platov into second place
and Usova and Zhulin into third, and reclaimed their old position
atop the podium for another richly deserved European Gold Medal.

Soon they would face the stiffest test of all - that elusive, all-
important Olympic Gold, which would be competed for by twenty
other couples representing countries from all over the world, not just
Europe. Top tips for a medal were then the Russian ice dancers who

had obtained, in the intervening years, a massive hold on the sport; there was also a strong contingent from the Ukraine, and other newly independent Eastern European countries including the Czech Republic and Hungary.

So, it was back to the drawing board. Every mark in the European Championship was carefully scrutinised and the judges' comments noted. Some of the costumes hadn't worked as we'd hoped and now had to be remade or adjusted. The stakes were high, but Jayne and Chris were perfectionists and never shied away from making any last-minute changes to obtain the ideal they always sought.

Now came the really difficult part of the whole project: to become the first skaters to return to the sport in which they had excelled, after ten years in an exceptionally successful professional career, and try to repeat their achievement with a second Olympic win. I stand to be corrected, but I cannot recall any previous gold medallists ever accomplishing such a feat. Nonetheless, they set themselves the task with their usual dedication and intelligence, constantly modifying, improving their technique and stamina, and tweaking every section.

When they travelled to Lillehammer to compete in the 1994 Winter Olympics Ice Dance event, (a competition and not, to everyone's surprise, a Championship), they were followed by an enormous press corps and even the practice sessions garnered huge audiences. Their Compulsory Dances would be the Starlight Waltz and the Blues; the Original Dance was once again, to be skated to a Rumba rhythm, with the final section to be the Free Dance. Nearly all these sections would be seen by a televised audience of millions across the world as well as being reported by the media at every step of the way.

When they stepped onto the ice to begin their comeback, their scores for the Compulsory Dances were disappointing, with a particularly low mark awarded by the Canadian judge for their Blues leaving them in third place.

The next morning, as they arrived for the early morning practice session for the Original Dance, they were devastated, almost to the point of abandoning the whole attempt, feeling that they'd been undermarked. All parties in their entourage then took part in a council of war. Bobby strongly advised them, as their Rumba was an outstanding example of pure perfection, it would have to be recognised by the judging panel. Luckily, they rather grudgingly agreed to practice for it, because there were hundreds of press and public in the practice rink, and I'm delighted to say that their Rumba was executed to delirious applause. It stopped them doubting their own ability, and that evening they skated it even better to win that section outright. They were back on track!

This was the year that Chris and Jayne were completely changing their Free Dance ethos, and their new routine had received many plaudits in the recent European Championships. It was another trial because in practice it had not been going well and some judges, who saw a chance of not placing them first in the final, smelt blood and a way they could support their own entries with impunity. Realising this, Jayne and Chris were determined to turn the tables on their detractors, although even their most fervent supporters were unsure of the Free Dance being up to their usual standard, given the practice sessions.

So, when the time came for them to take the ice and make Olympic history, our hearts were in our mouths. We needn't have worried. Staying with the monochrome theme, they appeared in skating versions of classic evening wear, a black suit and white shirt with black bowtie for Chris, in dramatic contrast to Jayne's shimmering silvery top and white skirt; and in all the years I'd been watching this partnership grow and mature, I can truly say I had never, never seen them skate so brilliantly. Every move, lift and step were perfectly executed, and the audience were wild with delight, clapping along to the lovely, exuberant music and raining bouquets onto the ice at the end. They must have won, surely?

Alas, no. They lost marks for technical merit on the grounds that some of their assisted jumps, (of which an unlimited number are permitted), counted as lifts, thereby exceeding the five allowed; the majority of judges awarded them 5.7, with the highest mark of 5.9 coming from Great Britain, and the lowest of 5.6 from Germany.

Amid boos and whistles from an outraged audience, the marks for interpretation appeared: a substantial improvement, with a 6.0 from the British judge, six marks of 5.9, and two of 5.8, but sadly not enough to win the Gold Medal many people felt they deserved. It went instead to the Russian pair, Oksana Grishuk and Evgeny Platov, and the Silver Medal to their compatriots Maya Usova and Alexander Zhulin. However, Chris and Jayne *did* win a standing ovation and their audience's hearts all over the world. There was a huge surge of support from the millions who had watched the final with bated breath; to their fans they were the winners even if they had to be satisfied with a Bronze Medal and the astonishing achievement of a podium place after a lapse of ten years.

From then on, their fame blossomed to become even greater than before, their professional career began afresh, and they travelled all over Great Britain for audiences to appreciate their wonderful talent - as they continue to this day with their popular *Dancing on Ice* TV show. Chris and Jayne's fame has now continued unabated for over thirty years and they're still doing what they love best, which must be an all-time record for any athletes.

Afterword

If Ice Dance had been an Olympic sport during his career, Courtney Jones would probably have been on two successive Olympic podiums with two different partners.

Without the trailblazers of the past there are no future champions - and Courtney helped pave the way for the force of British ice dancing, from the podium clean sweeps in 1955 – 56 and 1968 to Torvill and Dean becoming Olympic champions in 1984.

Courtney Jones was a true trailblazer in every way, a man of many talents and a passionate advocate of our sport throughout his long career on and off the ice. It has been a pleasure and privilege to share in his incredible story.

Photograph by The Headshot Box, courtesy of Robin Cousins, MBE

Robin Cousins, Vice-Chair and President of British Ice Skating

Acknowledgements and Gracias

I'd like to hem the tapestry of my life, as it were, by thanking some people without whose unstinting support this book would not have been written.

Of my collaborators, Peter Morrissey is probably the best known to the skating world as he is so well travelled. Now a judge, he has been a Board Member and General Secretary of the National Skating Association as well as past Honorary Secretary of the British Ice Teachers Association. A tower of strength from the beginning of this odyssey, I've known Peter since he was a young man, and as he had a home near us in Spain when I started this project, he was with me from Day One. His enthusiasm was infectious throughout the months that followed, his knowledge has been invaluable, and I thank him for his many contributions and guidance.

Elaine Hooper is another old friend from the skating community who, over the past decades, has always assisted me when planning my charity projects and championships - the perfect 'Backroom Girl'! I am so happy that her dedication to our sport has now been internationally recognised by her appointment by British Ice Skating to be their Official Historian, with colleagues from all over the world now asking her advice. Elaine has been a rock throughout; no query from me or my collaborators, large or small, has ever failed to get an immediate reply to make my narrative technically correct. Thank you.

Heather Jones is no relation, though I wish she were! We were introduced by Julie, a mutual friend, while I was making stumbling efforts to write but my grammar was poor. Heather, a very proficient administrator, endlessly corrected my punctuation and as she too became interested in the text, we spent many hours on the telephone correcting my writings. Heather's bubbly personality kept me focussed throughout the twelve-week lockdown and made me concentrate on the job in hand. She kept my spirits up during the following months with her conviction that our efforts *would* be published - and she was right! Thank you, too.

Helen Cox, my editor, publisher, and recent good and long-suffering friend, also spent endless hours trying to turn my memories into a viable document and encouraging me to continue telling my story - I shall forever be in her debt for her unflagging enthusiasm and knowledge. We were introduced through a very strange coincidence, as she will explain:

'Courtney and I met via our mutual friend Ron, a long-standing customer of my husband Mick's gardening business. For many years Ron and his family had a holiday home in Spain, where they met Courtney and Bobby; and when Courtney mentioned that he was writing his memoirs but had no clue about how to get them published, to my eternal gratitude, Ron said that he knew a local writer back home who might be able to help.

I was happy to do so if I could, and in March 2020 Courtney and I began discussing his options by email and phone. He kindly sent me several extracts, including 'John Curry' and 'Lunch with The Queen,' which I read with great interest and a strong feeling that he should forget about self-publishing and offer it to a mainstream publisher who could give it the treatment it deserved. It was a great story and Courtney had a great gift for telling it - although as a teacher in junior school once remarked in my English report, 'the style is somewhat in conflict with the content.' I didn't realise that not only had he never attempted any major writing project before, he was a complete novice with computers; but undeterred by such obstacles, had set about mastering the unfamiliar technology to produce well over sixty thousand words. Clearly written with increasing ease and fluency as the months passed and he became more practised, this seemed a long work indeed to its author – but he took it in remarkably good part when I told him that, as autobiographies go, it was in fact quite short; and ever obliging, penned another ten thousand words.

In early 2021, Courtney emailed his first approach to a publisher. A month later, he copied the proposal to me and asked whether it was normal to wait so long for a reply. Having had long experience in preparing my own and other peoples' work for publication, I thought I knew why he had failed to elicit a response - and what was needed to make it succeed. I also knew it would take infinitely longer to explain how to Courtney than to simply do it myself, and in view of the exciting developments coming up in British and international skating, there was no time to waste. I accordingly volunteered my services and awaited his reply in some trepidation lest it seemed offensive or presumptuous.

He demurred at first in the mistaken belief that it was too huge a task for a new penfriend to take on. I assured him that on the contrary, working round other commitments, I could crack it in three months. After discussing the matter with Bobby, to my great joy he then accepted, and off we went. I received batches of the original text by email from Courtney and from Heather, who also sent me a thick wad of hard copy, (some of which I transcribed directly, editing as I went). The material ranged from notes and early drafts to polished anecdotes and narrative passages both long and short requiring little or no alteration; it had holes that needed filling with facts, largely furnished by Elaine, and threadbare patches to embroider with details, largely furnished by Courtney in response to my lists of questions; and since not everything was arranged chronologically, it was going to take a lot of unpicking and re-stitching to weave all these elements into a seamless length ready for public display.

I immediately tore in with gusto. The problem was less finding time for the work than stopping for anything else; so first and foremost, I must thank my beloved, long-suffering husband Mick Doggett, who for three months saw more of the cat than of me in our marital bed as I spent so many nights feverishly editing, and as a result, so many evenings crashed out on the couch after dinner.

To help me arrange the sections in the right order, I needed to know more about the general shape of Courtney's life. Slightly too young to remember his heyday on ice, I'd long been aware, albeit unwittingly, of his work – Torvill and Dean's marvellous 'Bolero' and 'Paso Doble' costumes, for instance, and the emergence of outsize fashion from its ignominious hiding-place at the back of the store to prominence in the marketplace. A quick internet trawl led me to skateguard1.blogspot.com and Ryan Stevens' 'Choctaws, Costumes and Charisma: the Courtney Jones Story,' which I found incredibly useful (as were other skating history blogs on the site). I subsequently contacted Ryan via Facebook regarding, I hoped, the impending publication of *Around The Ice*, and with his kind permission, gratefully acknowledge this fascinating blog and commend it to readers.

The proverbial mine of information, thanks to her inside-out knowledge of world skating and access to substantial archives, Elaine Hooper always found the answer to queries ranging from the history of Westover Ice Rink to recipients of the John Davis Trophy. She also provided masses of background information, and minutely combed successive drafts, correcting my myriad mistakes and misunderstandings. I learnt a huge amount from her, and wholeheartedly add my thanks to Courtney's for her invaluable help in making this book as factually correct as possible. Likewise, Peter Morrissey, whose painstaking attention spotted several overlooked errors, and whose helpful suggestions as an experienced author in the field have made aspects of the text more accessible to an international readership. As a newcomer to this genre, I found it tremendously reassuring to know that everything would be vetted by their expert eyes before going to print, and I'm extremely grateful to them both.

Heather also deserves a special mention for her superb proof-reading skills and constructive suggestions for changes and improvements, including an interesting expansion on the name 'Courtney,' and for pointing out numerous placename and geographical errors it never occurred to me to check. Heather's enthusiastic praise for my efforts and eager demands for the next instalment were always a great confidence booster, and a great spur to crack on with the work. For someone who normally writes alone, this was all a rare treat; Courtney generously referred to the project as 'our book,' and that's just how it felt: a team of interested volunteers pooling resources to bring a worthy project to fruition, and I enjoyed being a part of it more than I can say. Thank you, everyone, for welcoming me into your world.

As the weft grew and the picture resolved, the massive impact of Courtney's amazing talents on skating and fashion over many decades finally hit home. Blushing at my ignorance and the memory of the email lectures I'd inflicted on this eminent person, I watched footage of his winning performances, and of other champions featured in these pages, relishing them even more with my newly informed eyes. I can't claim it was a dream come true to correspond with three of my all-time skating heroes, (the fourth being the late John Curry), because my subconscious had never remotely conceived such a thing. So it was a most thrilling surprise to find myself doing so, and I feel deeply grateful to Robin Cousins for taking the time to reply to an obscure stranger's questions, allowing quotes from his personal emails, and supplying the Afterword, cover quote and portrait; also to Christopher Dean and Jayne Torvill for their Foreword; and to Jayne's husband Phil Christensen, for providing its superb illustration and obtaining photographer Alfie Hitchcock's generous permission to reproduce it in a form which, alas, completely fails to do justice to the original.

When it became clear that the only way of ensuring the book was on the market by 2022 was to publish it though Herstory, the team rose as one to meet the new challenges presented by self-publication. Courtney trawled through his albums for suitable photographs; Elaine helped with the cover design, sourced images, obtained copyright permissions, and spread word of the impending publication on social media (as did Ryan Stevens); Peter and Heather also helped with photographs and presentation choices. Also, Duncan Beal, Paula Charles and their colleagues at York Publishing Services (YPS), the company who have produced all my previous books, did a marvellous job to expedite the process, and I'm very grateful for the speed with which they got us into print

Finally, I'd like to thank the man who made all this possible, the inimitable Courtney Jones – and Bobby Thompson - from the bottom of my heart. Letting me loose on their precious words was a great act of trust and far from long-suffering, I consider myself the luckiest writer alive. *Around The Ice* is easily the most important editing job I've ever done (or ever will, I suspect) – it's been an incredible journey through an incredible story, and I only hope I've done it justice. Thank you so much for giving me this unique opportunity, dear Courtney. It's been a most rewarding experience in every way, and I've loved every minute.'

Sadly, due to the Covid restrictions in force while this book was in production, some of us have never had chance to meet in the flesh – so as a final stitch in my tapestry I raise a glass to you all, to the time when we can do so freely. CHEERS! It's been great fun.

Adieu, dear readers.

Courtney Jones

THANK YOU, LADIES AND GENTLEMEN. NOW PLEASE LEAVE THE ICE!

Other Herstory Publications:

Non-fiction by Helen Cox:

The Battle of Wakefield Revisited: a fresh perspective on Richard of York's final battle, December 1460
Walk Wakefield 1460: A Visitor Guide to Battle-Related Sites
Walk Towton 1461: A Visitor Guide to Battle-Related Sites (co-author Alan Stringer)

Fiction by Rae Andrew:

The Lay of Angor Book 1: Gondarlan
The Lay of Angor Book 2: Breath of Gaia
The Lay of Angor Book 3: Wolfsbane
Henry Wowler & the Mirror-Cat (for children)

Forthcoming:

An Accidental Kitten: The Tail of Henry Wowler
The Lay of Angor, revised single volume 2nd edition in English and French